CULTURE, LEARNING, AND THE DISCIPLINES

CULTURE, LEARNING, AND THE DISCIPLINES

THEORY AND PRACTICE IN CROSS-CULTURAL ORIENTATION

EDITED BY

JOSEF A. MESTENHAUSER
GAYLA MARTY
INGE STEGLITZ

NAFSA

National Association for Foreign Student Affairs
Washington, D.C.

ISBN 0-912207-23-X

Contents

Preface

Most of the chapters in this book were presented as papers at an invitational conference on orientation in Minneapolis in November 1984 conducted under the auspices of the Council on International Educational Exchange, the International Society for Educational, Cultural and Scientific Interchanges, and Region IV of the National Association for Foreign Student Affairs (NAFSA). The cooperation of these sponsors brought together orientation practitioners and scholars to consider each others' needs and experiences. The United States Information Agency (USIA) provided financial assistance that enabled overseas scholars and practitioners to attend, thus placing the conference and resulting publications in a truly international context. The entire field of international educational exchange has been enriched by USIA's vision in supporting not only the conference, but also NAFSA's Field Service program, whose steering committee was especially helpful in recommending this project for publication.

This book is the last in a series of publications resulting from the 1984 conference. The first volume (Paige 1986) dealt with theoretical concepts on which cross-cultural orientation programs are based, while the second volume, a special journal issue (Martin 1986), focused on training perspectives. Three articles were published separately (Kohls 1987, Christopher 1987, and Hughes-Wiener 1987). Two of the chapters in this volume were adapted from theses inspired by the conference (Steglitz and Rosenquist Watts).

The conference's joint steering committee, composed of representatives of the sponsoring groups, organized the conference and also served as the editorial committee that helped select papers for publication. Members were Jon Booth, Josef Mestenhauser, and Michael Paige from the University of Minnesota, and David Sanford from Macalaster College in St. Paul.

The senior editor benefited greatly from a professional opportunity in Indonesia, designing a cross-cultural predeparture orientation program for Indonesian scholars going to study in Western countries. The project, which helped focus on the need to integrate cross-cultural orientation with language and academic achievement, was sponsored by the Midwestern

Universities Consortium for International Activities with funding from the Agency for International Development.

The editors also wish to express their appreciation to the authors for their generous cooperation throughout the extended formation of this book. Finally, the manuscript would not have seen the light of day without the expert processing skills of Adele Bergstrom, who provided the glue for this difficult task.

JOSEPH A. MESTENHAUSER
GAYLA MARTY
INGE STEGLITZ

Minneapolis, Minnesota
January 1988

Introduction

Orientation is perhaps the one thing all members of the National Association for Foreign Student Affairs (NAFSA) have in common. We orient U.S. students for study abroad, foreign students who come to study in the United States, the faculty and staff who work with both these groups; foreign teaching assistants who teach U.S. students; students of English as a second language; and community and host families who provide home-stay and enrichment programs. In a broader sense, we also orient new members to the profession; newly elected or appointed leaders to their NAFSA responsibilities; our bosses—about the complexity of our work and the need for more funding; specific audiences, such as campus religious groups, community businesses, governmental agencies, sponsors, prospective employers; and a host of others. Overseas advisers conduct orientation programs for our prospective foreign students and often orient U.S. students who become foreign students abroad. Admissions officers participate in these orientation programs, orient overseas advisers, write handouts and brochures, evaluate credentials that orient students to differences in educational systems; and their materials in turn create expectations that influence students' adjustment.

There are, then, many "orientations," many solutions, and many objectives—all based on different perceptions and uses of the word. This has led some authors to distinguish between "briefing," "orientation," "training," and "education" (Kohls 1987, J. Bennett 1986). According to these distinctions, the more objectives we develop and the more complex they become, the further we move on the scale from briefing into education.

We also know that orientation is effective. Grove and Torbiörn (1986) concluded persuasively that appropriate prearrival and suitably reinforced host-country post-arrival orientation can shorten adjustment from 7.9 units to 3.8 units of time. Similarly, Bachner and Blohm (1986), researching the impact of orientation in the Japan project of the Youth for Understanding (YFU) program, concluded that it actually determined the success of the program. The Peace Corps (Nicholson, Chapter 14) has spent some twenty million dollars on orientation training from recruitment to return for some 100,000 volunteers. That is about $200 per person. Our public policy recognizes that a high degree of success in a risky enterprise demands professional services. Can you imagine what we could do if public policy accorded the same significance and priority to educational exchanges? Mumford Fowler's chapter (Chapter 15) reinforces this message. She provides a dramatic example of how orientation saved military lives in Vietnam, and how similar Navy human-relations programs in Puerto Rico improved morale and efficiency on the job and decreased absenteeism as well as negative incidents between local citizens and sailors on the base. In addition, it improved relations between husbands, wives, and children. None of the above deal with college students, however. This is why the present volume includes different client groups: counseling and orientation for U.S. and foreign students is often directed toward the same broad results, whether documented or not.

At the same time, there is no common expectation about what orientation should be and who should do it. Paradoxically, this was one of the reasons for the success of the Minneapolis conference: many people were engaged in orientation, but most were uncertain about how well they were doing it and wanted to learn more. Mumford Fowler observed there that there was no common expected outcome of orientation, and no easy way to know when individuals became "oriented." She found it difficult to improve Navy programs when criticisms were voiced because there was no accepted yardstick by which to evaluate a program's effectiveness. Because of this the programs lacked an institutional base and funds, completing the cycle of indecision—she termed this the Navy's equivalent of academia's "absence of decision."

A second major problem in orientation is motivation. Steglitz attributes it to "the nature of the clientele": too little time, too much pressure, too many distractions with other demands, inadequate understanding of the language, information overload causing inability to absorb newness, and many other factors. Still, although logistics present a formidable barrier, Koester suggests that *when students are motivated to learn, they do so* (Chapter 16). Campus practitioners should also look very carefully at Nicholson's contribution (Chapter 14): he describes not only the kind of training given to Peace Corps participants, but suggests that their experiences showed the complete irrelevance of "academic models" of orientation used in the early years of the corps. It has since rejected these models in favor of experiential theories, which appear to be suitable not only for survival but for task-oriented functioning.

These two issues—the lack of agreement on standards for orientation, and the common lack of motivation to attend—form the questions for this book. Can we all improve our conceptual understanding of cross-cultural learning and transfer of knowledge, so we can realize maximum effectiveness from the efforts we do make? This book is a step in that direction. Can we develop more sophisticated handbooks for students that relate orientation and preparation more directly to their personal, academic, and professional goals? Mumford Fowler suggests that self-directed readings work. Can we obtain more support from teaching faculty? Clarke has demonstrated that it is possible. Can we develop a network on an international level that will synchronize orientation in the home country with orientation in the host country? Some modest efforts are already being made in this direction with overseas educational advisers, whose membership in NAFSA offers us exceptional opportunities to work together in projects that go beyond recruiting. There is considerable attention being paid to cross-cultural orientation in Europe (Winter 1986; Danckwortt 1985) and in Canada (Hawes & Kealey 1979; Westwood, Lawrence & McBlane 1986).

This book is not an orientation handbook. NAFSA practitioners have rich resources in handbooks, such as those produced by the Experiment in International Living (EIL) and AFS International/Intercultural. AFS has published them annually since 1981, and Alvino Fantini wrote an outstanding handbook published by EIL in 1984. Most Fulbright commissions abroad also produce orientation guides; the most comprehensive and conceptually rich was recently released by the Japan-U.S. Educational Commission (1987). Individual colleges have produced in-house materials and handbooks, the most comprehensive being one by Parandeh Kia (1986) at Ohio University in Athens. A unique orientation handbook by the Board for International Food and Agricultural Development (BIFAD) of the U.S. Agency for International Development is available in loose-leaf edition, but only to Title XII readers, most at land-grant institutions participating in agricultural development (McArthur et al. 1984). NAFSA itself regularly publishes handbooks on specific aspects of international educational exchange; the most recent relevant to orientation is Patricia Burak's work on crisis counseling (1987). The Peace Corps, the U.S. Navy, and Youth for Understanding all have manuals, but unfortunately these are unpublished.

Rather than standing as a manual on its own, the present book is a companion to these other publications. It attempts a unique blend of major cross-cultural learning and training issues, written primarily by NAFSAns.

The first and most significant contribution this book makes is to the marriage of theory and practice. It is a marriage of reason rather than love, however; we might not have undertaken this task had we realized how difficult it would be! We all are familiar with the frustration of theoreticians and researchers who often do not know how to translate ideas into programs, and of practitioners who have difficulty knowing how theory is supposed to underpin their activities. This common problem—in effect a problem of transfer of knowledge—is demonstrated in Steglitz's and Rosenquist Watts's survey chapters. They asked practitioners about their awareness and knowledge of selected concepts and learned that not only do organizers of orientation programs not utilize many of these theories, but many are not familiar with them. This volume strives to overcome the criticism many cross-cultural publications and research suffer, that never the twain—theory and practice—shall meet.

Second, as indicated above, this book brings materials from less familiar sources, such as the Peace Corps, military agencies, foreign service establishments, development agencies, business corporations, and even travel agencies. Although this volume does not include contributions from community volunteers, the corporate world, and development work, whose important programs are less common or unpublicized, we suspect they would reinforce the examples here. Academic practitioners need to be aware of what others are doing and to recognize that cross-cultural education is a growing field, that we are not alone in this area, and that there are many common denominators for all of us despite the differences in our "client populations." Although foreign service institutes and corporations do not publish their cross-cultural orientation materials and methods, there is evidence that their activities—and the sophistication of those activities—are increasing. We have a long way to go, and we can learn from them.

An important third point of this book is that working with foreign and U.S. students forms two sides of the same coin. The authors represented in this volume utilize the same concepts and theories, describe the educational process in the same terms, and subscribe to the same goals and objectives. Furthermore, foreign and U.S. students participate in orientation programs for each other for the same reasons: they learn from the experiences of others. Despite some apparent differences, both groups are concerned with learning a foreign language, and both need the same important skills, including cultural sensitivity, cross-cultural communication, flexibility, adjustability, and the ability to make inferences based on incomplete knowledge of host cultures. Any differences, we feel, are superficial and often of our own making, depending on the ways our campuses are organized. For these and several other reasons that will become more apparent later in the book, we focus on orientation for both of these important populations, U.S. and foreign students.

Readers will be pleased to notice that the students described here, especially the U.S. students, are concerned with issues beyond immediate skill acquisition. Many know intuitively or explicitly that the world is becoming interdependent, and that they will have to learn, in addition to occupational skills, how to understand the world around them. This relates directly to the fourth aim of this volume: the professionalization of our field. Educational exchanges are again considered an important medium for accomplishing goals beyond the immediate and practical for individuals and their organizations. Felsing's and Rosenquist Watts's chapters (Chapters 10 and 9) indicate that for many NAFSAns, orientation is of relatively recent vintage; on the other hand, O'Driscoll's and Baker's contributions (Chapters 2 and 12) trace orientation to the beginning of modern educational exchanges, developed primarily as an adjunct to cultural diplomacy—an idea that in recent years appears to have been lost to concerns with individual adjustment and corporate and product competitiveness. We might be surprised to learn that chaplains started the Navy's program as a humanitarian endeavor, not unlike the religious efforts of missionaries who accompanied early educational exchange personnel in China and the Philippines.

Today we will enhance the importance of our work, of orientation programs, and of our own professional standing if we revive and enhance the emphasis on international relations and understanding and on development education. Professionalism provides not only high quality critical services to individual clients, but contributes to the larger society. This broader goal is what distinguishes professionals from business people, whose goal is oriented toward profit, and from bureaucrats, whose goal is to administer rules and regulations. This book aims to support NAFSA and NAFSAns as a primary force in international and intercultural education and training. Byrd (Chapter 6) saw an interesting relevance between professionalism and the need to upgrade the qualifications of English as a second language teachers in cross-cultural skills; she applauded those who took initiative in training and re-training themselves, and attributed their enthusiastic response to professional development opportunities to the fact that ESL is in an energetic stage of becoming a profession. The same can be true for international education practitioners.

The reader should therefore not be surprised to find that this book presents an interdisciplinary and holistic picture, despite the inclusion of several chapters with limited objectives. Even if it is not a simple handbook, it should be very useful to almost any practitioner. To those with limited orientation goals or resources, these chapters show how much can be done if efforts are well organized and orchestrated into cooperative programs. For those interested in sustained education and the resulting synergy, this work can inform and inspire: they may be sufficiently energized to increase their own training competence, minimize repetition, increase the levels of program sophistication, improve their ability to articulate the need for orientation (thus justifying more tangible fiscal support), and sharpen publicity to help increase the motivation of the "clients" to attend.

The book begins with the specific and the practical—that is how experiential learning works. Steglitz and Rosenquist Watts introduce the first and last halves of Part I with chapters describing what colleges and universities do in orientation programs for foreign students (Chapter 1) and U.S. students (Chapter 9).

The first half of Part I is devoted to orientation programs for foreign students coming to the United States. O'Driscoll (Chapter 2) provides an interesting historical perspective on the Fulbright orientation programs, showing how initial attempts at political socialization were quickly changed to broad objectives of cultural diplomacy. In this vein, Sarles (Chapter 3) provides a cross-cultural perspective on interpreting U.S. life and culture to incoming Fulbright scholars. He demonstrates the synergy of international education: students coming here must have a minimum functional understanding of our culture, which can be provided convincingly and credibly if done with cultural sensitivity and a comparative perspective; at the same time, such orientation contributes to the students' new insights about their own cultures, which in turn produces not only a higher level of understanding, but also a functional and rapid adjustment, avoiding costly negative attributions and stereotypical thinking. (Supporting the need to interpret the life and culture of the United States cross-culturally are two worthy references by Kohls [1988, to be published by NAFSA and Intercultural Press] and Vetter [1983].) Kuhlman and Cadman (Chapters 4 and 5) contribute very elegant accounts of foreign student orientations, one on the campus of a major university, the other in Washington, D.C. on behalf of a national program sponsored by the United States Agency for International Development. Byrd and Landa (Chapters 6 and 7) deal with orientation in the context of English language training, one for beginners in intensive institutes and the other in programs for foreign teaching assistants. Byrd draws a parallel between such intensive institutes and "half-way houses," a common metaphor used for orientation programs in general—as if they were "decompression chambers" along the way to somewhere else. Conceptually, this suggests that an orientation program is an agency of socialization for a stay in another culture, for which students from multiple countries have no other common preparation. Landa also raises a critical issue, noting that the learning objectives in making foreign students effective teachers are determined more by outside forces than by the "clients" themselves. We are confronted with a graft between technical and cultural skills, then grafted again with social psychological variables of perceptions and attitudes. Gamboa (Chapter 8) portrays a campus orientation retreat based on experiential theories. It is an excellent evaluation scheme that utilizes an innovative set of variables—worth duplicating elsewhere.

The second half of Part I is devoted to orientation for Americans, including youth, students, Peace Corps volunteers, and military personnel. Felsing (Chapter 10) offers a delightful example of an eclectic model, unabashedly discussing the small steps preceding a larger leap. Clarke (Chapter 11) describes not only a special format of orientation—a retreat—but the confluence of many resources with academic and non-academic goals. The third campus-based program, by Baker (Chapter 12), contains a "three-tiered" approach that is an excellent practical example of a triple graft, to which we return in Part II. Soquet (Chapter 13) shows how orientation is applicable to various audiences, including, in her case, participants in youth exchanges. She places orientation programs squarely in the arena of Maslowian theories of actuation, development, and growth. Her organization, the Experiment in International Living, has also produced some of the best handbooks for orientation, and has pioneered the experiential learning approach based on adult learning theories, known as andragogy. Nicholson and Mumford Fowler (Chapters 14 and 15) describe the government programs mentioned earlier. Finally, Koester (Chapter 16) provides a rich topping to Part I. She is a former exchange participant who first became a practitioner, then an academician and researcher in communication. Her research is an outstanding example of evaluation that is providing basic knowledge to the field but also has immediate practical relevance, especially to orientation and motivation for study abroad. Another of her studies makes a major contribution to needs assessment as a basis of orientation (Koester 1985, 1987).

Virtually every chapter makes references to some form of evaluation of previous programs, no matter how simple these may be. The most dramatic example is described by Mumford Fowler in connection with an attitude survey of some 55,000 Marines; their widely held stereotypes provided a rationale for an extensive orientation program whose results and outcomes were spectacular. Perhaps the most sophisticated example is referenced in Nicholson's chapter, in which he explains that the Peace Corps's present orientation programs are results of detailed analysis of every single task in which volunteers engaged on every day of their activities. Unfortunately, this research is not accessible to the public. Gamboa and Koester (Chapters 8 and 16) reveal the significance of research and evaluation not only for the purpose of knowing how well we are doing, but especially to gain an understanding of how our practical solutions to orientation relate to the concepts and theories. Of course, the evaluations represent experiences of others, and as we know, personal experience is the basis of all learning; but this does not minimize the need to produce research that also documents the effectiveness of orientation programs.

After reading the fourteen chapters about specific orientation programs, the reader should not be misled into believing that these programs do not have any theoretical underpinning, even if the authors occasionally make such disclaimers. They are using theories and concepts even if they do not recognize them. The first theoretical considerations made by all contributors to this book are various learning concepts and theories. These are relevant to decisions about orientation's timing, instructional strategies, selection of content, sequencing of materials, methods of presentation, use of resources, learning outcomes, expectations of participants, motivation to attend, involvement of others in the process, and the importance of orientation to the subsequent sojourn in a foreign culture. The most important treatment of these learning assumptions is found, curiously, in the chapters describing orientation programs that are sponsored by large national organizations, especially the Experiment in International Living, Peace Corps, and the U.S. Navy. This really should not be surprising, because campus-based practitioners appear to come primarily from the counseling-based programs in which orientation is common. Their theoretical background is taken from psychological developmental theories and from concepts dealing with the impact of social change on individuals, the adjustments needed to be made, and the stress to be dealt with when people are in transition and need support, acceptance, and coping skills (Maslow 1954).

Another set of theoretical assumptions is made about culture as a major variable of adjustment. Every chapter in this book deals with cultural differences and similarities, comparison of host and home cultures, and the uniqueness or universality of values in both. Many make implicit and explicit assumptions about the need to know one's own culture as a condition of acquiring insight on another culture. "Culture shock" is the one concept familiar not only to the authors, but to the general practitioners surveyed. In fact, the concept is so common that we find it even in tourist guides (e.g., American Womens' Association, 1975).

In Part II, we attempt to bring the practice and theory together. Chapter 17 explains why we have problems applying theory to programs. There are simply too many of these concepts and theories, and they come from several distinct disciplines that traditionally have not been brought together in our academic training and in the preparation of professionals in our field. Even people familiar with these social and behavioral science concepts often experience difficulties because the concepts must be "grafted" onto one another. Four chapters in this volume (O'Driscoll, Byrd, Landa, and Koester) demonstrate that the graft involves not two but three stems: foreign language, foreign culture, and the field of study or task to be performed.

The phenomenon of culture shock provides an example of how important concepts are to orientation, and how the grafting of these concepts works. In culture shock, the first graft is between learning concepts and culture theories. In other words, culture shock is a result of an encounter with another culture whose cognitive structure differs from ours. Now put this in the context of specialized support services provided by skilled human relations professionals, who will help ease the disequilibrium resulting from culture shock. Conceptually, these services are based on psychological developmental theories, which suggest that basic needs must be satisfied before a person can function in another culture. The third stem to be grafted then relates to those basic needs, the tasks for which people go to other cultures, most commonly to study a subject matter, to conduct research, to grow personally and professionally, to acquire another language, or to understand other people. We might also call this the product an individual wants to obtain through the sojourn. Even if we organize orientation programs for very limited objectives, such as immediate resettlement in another culture, it is clear that we cannot think of orientation without thinking about the entire educational experience abroad. It is as if orientation were a button that, when touched, rings many doorbells in many places and at many times.

The principal bias of this book, then, is that any orientation (or even simple briefing) is very valuable to newcomers to any culture. On the other hand, professionals who aspire to be educators miss their calling if they function merely as "process people," no matter how important that task may be in itself. To be an educator, one must be able to conceptualize the entire cross-cultural experience, because orientation is its process from beginning to end. Accordingly, we will end by suggesting a new model of orientation, which in turn might create its own new practice.

Let us now proceed to what practitioners have done in organizing various orientation programs, how they solved logistical, financial, pedagogical, and motivational problems, how they have dealt with the cultural variables, and how they assess the effectiveness of orientation programs.

References

American Field Service. 1981. *AFS orientation handbook*, first edition. New York: AFS International/Intercultural Programs, Inc.

_____. 1982. *AFS orientation handbook*, second edition. New York: AFS International/Intercultural Programs, Inc.

_____. 1983. *AFS orientation handbook*, third edition. New York: AFS International/Intercultural Programs, Inc.

_____. 1984. *AFS orientation handbook volume IV*. New York: AFS International/Intercultural Programs, Inc.

_____. 1985. *AFS orientation handbook volume V*. New York: AFS International/Intercultural Programs, Inc.

American Women's Association. 1975. *Introducing Indonesia*. New Jakarta: P.T. INTERMASA.

Bachner, David J. and Judith M. Blohm. 1986. Orienting U.S. student sojourners to

Japan: Content, approach, and implications. In R. Michael Paige, ed., *Cross-cultural orientation: New conceptualizations and applications.* Lanham, MD: University Press of America.

Bennett, Janet M. 1986. Modes of cross-cultural training: Conceptualizing cross-cultural training as education. *International Journal of Intercultural Relations* (10)2.

Burak, Patricia A. 1987. *Crisis management in a cross-cultural setting.* Washington, D.C.: NAFSA.

Christopher, Elizabeth. 1987. Academia: A cross-cultural problem. *International Journal of Intercultural Relations* 11(2):191–206.

Danckwortt, Dieter. 1985. *Intercultural learning: Conference documents.* International Conference on Intercultural Learning. Bonn, West Germany: Deutsche Stiftung für internationale Entwicklung.

Fantini, Alvino E., ed. 1984. *Cross-cultural orientation: A guide for leaders and educators.* Brattleboro, VT: The Experiment in International Living.

Grove, Cornelius Lee and Ingemar Torbiörn. 1986. A new conceptualization of intercultural adjustment and the goals of learning. In R. Michael Paige, ed., *Cross-cultural orientation: New conceptualizations and applications.* Lanham: University Press of America.

Hawes, Frank and Daniel J. Kealey. September 1979. Canadians in development: An empirical study of adaptation and effectiveness on overseas assignment. A Technical Report. Canadian International Development Agency.

Hughes-Wiener, Gail. 1986. The "learning how to learn" approach to cross-cultural orientation. *International Journal of Intercultural Relations* (10)4.

The Japan-United States Educational Commission. 1987. *Pre-departure orientation handbook.* Tokyo, Japan: The Japan-United States Educational Commission.

Kia, Parandeh. 1986. A manual for international student orientation coordinators. Athens, Ohio, Ohio University. Unpublished manuscript.

Koester, Jolene. 1985. *A profile of the U.S. student abroad.* New York: Council on International Educational Exchange.

_____. 1987. *A profile of the U.S. student abroad—1984 and 1985.* New York: Council on International Educational Exchange.

Kohls, L. Robert. 1987. Four traditional approaches to developing cross-cultural preparedness in adults: Education, training, orientation, and briefing. *International Journal of Inter-cultural Relations* 11(1):89–106.

_____. 1988. Models for comparing and contrasting cultures. In Joy Reid, ed., *Building professional dimensions of educational exchange.* Yarmouth, ME: Intercultural Press, Inc.

McArthur, Harold et al., eds. 1984. *Designing orientation and project support programs for overseas technical assistance personnel: A handbook for university administrators and managers.* Manoa, Hawaii: University of Hawaii at Manoa, for the Board of International Food and Agricultural Development, U.S.A.I.D., Washington, D.C.

Martin, Judith N., ed. 1986. Theories and methods in cross-cultural orientation. *In-*

ternational *Journal of Intercultural Relations* 10(2).

Maslow, Abraham H. 1954. *Motivation and personality*. New York: Harper and Row.

National Association for Foreign Student Affairs. 1980. *Orientation of foreign students*. Guideline Series 4. Washington, D.C.: NAFSA.

_____. 1979. *Study abroad: Handbook for advisers and administrators*. Washington, D.C.: Field Service Program, NAFSA.

_____. April, 1975. *SECUSSA sourcebook: A guide for advisers of U.S. students planning an overseas experience*. Washington, D.C.: NAFSA.

_____. April, 1972. *An inquiry into departmental policies and practices in relation to the graduate education of foreign students*. Washington, D.C.: Field Service Program, NAFSA.

_____. 1964. Guidelines—initial orientation of foreign students. Field Service Publications, NAFSA. Washington, D.C.: NAFSA.

_____. 1949. *Handbook for counselors of students from abroad, experimental 1949 edition*. New York: NAFSA.

Paige, R. Michael, ed. 1986. *Cross-cultural orientation: New conceptualizations and applications*. Lanham, MD: University Press of America.

Vetter, Charles T. Jr. 1983. *Citizen ambassadors*. Provo, UT: Brigham Young University Center for International and Area Studies.

Westwood, M.J., Scott Lawrence, and Rorri McBlane. 1986. New dimensions in orientation of international students. In R. Michael Paige, ed., *Cross-cultural orientation: New conceptualizations and applications*. Lanham, MD: University Press of America.

Winter, Gerhard. 1986. German-American student exchange: Adaptation problems and opportunities for personal growth. In R. Michael Paige, ed., *Cross-cultural orientation: New conceptualizations and applications*. Lanham, MD: University Press of America.

PART ONE

Orientation Programs

Orientation for
International Students

1

Survey of University Orientation Programs for International Students and Scholars

Inge Steglitz

The conference on orientation programs sponsored by the Council on International Educational Exchange, the International Society for Educational, Scientific and Cultural Interchange, and the National Association for Foreign Student Affairs (NAFSA) in November 1984 produced new information on state-of-the-art orientation programs, as reflected in the chapters of this volume. But it also brought up new questions. The editorial team sensed there was more going on in the everyday practice of international student orientation than the papers showed, but more detailed information was needed.

We developed a questionnaire to assess orientation activities and, in September 1985, sent it to 600 international student advising offices across the country, all at colleges enrolling at least 100 foreign students (NAFSA Census, 1983–84). It was designed around these guiding questions:

1. What is actually being done in orientation programs?
2. What role do theoretical concepts play in the development and execution of orientation programs? (This dimension was conspicuously lacking in most of the conference papers.)
3. What do practitioners think *should* be done?

By February 1986, 169 questionnaires had been returned. However, because most were not filled out completely, we analyzed only 14 of the 26 questions—namely, those answered by most of the 169 respondents. We also included some information on the institutional context of orientation programs.

What Is Being Done in Orientation Programs?

The practitioners were asked to list and rank the five most important goals and objectives of their programs. The responses fell roughly into 11

5

TABLE 1

Most Important Goals and Objectives

Rank	1	2	3	4	5	Total
Categories						
Academic/administrative rules & regulations; registration	51	59	36	18	13	177[a]
Campus/community welcome	26	18	26	26	24	120
Services on- and off-campus	5	7	24	26	26	88
Adjustment to the U.S.	16	17	6	16	14	69
Immigration & Naturalization Service	8	9	20	10	11	58
Locations	10	16	11	12	4	53
Immediate needs	13	10	9	4	12	48
Introduction to international student advising office	15	5	9	12	2	43
Intercultural communication	8	3	5	9	8	33
English and other tests	3	5	4	4	3	19
Miscellaneous	8	14	13	17	13	65
TOTAL	163[b]	163[b]	163[b]	154[c]	130[d]	773

[a] Some practitioners listed more than one goal in this category.
[b] Out of 169 questionnaires, six did not answer these questions.
[c] Nine did not list more than three goals for their programs.
[d] Twenty-four did not list more than four goals for their programs.

categories of varying concreteness (see Table 1). The miscellaneous category included "prearrival information," "improve financial management and decision-making skills," "create an awareness of future orientation programs on culture shock, etc.," "education on safety," "increase the awareness of health and safety issues," "make friends in the U.S.," "academic skills," and "introduce U.S. students to other cultures."

As Table 1 shows, academic/administrative requirements and registration rank first in importance as orientation objectives, representing 23 percent of the total objectives listed. Practitioners also pay attention to students' psychological well-being, reflected in the campus/community welcome category (15.5% of the total listings). Assuming that priority determines what practitioners will do first, this may predict the sequencing of orientation programs.

From a list of topics compiled from the literature and our own experience, respondents were asked to identify topics their programs included (see Table 2). Most of the topics on the list were identified by more than 50 percent of the respondents. A quarter of the respondents used the "other" category, most often to refer to social activities. The overall response to this question supported the emerging picture that orientation is most often

TABLE 2

Topics Included in Programs

Topics	No. of Programs	% of Totals[a]
Visa/Immigration Service	159	94.6
Registration procedures	154	91.7
Health services	151	90.0
Academic advising	141	83.9
Housing	134	79.8
Finances/banking	131	78.0
Campus programs	125	74.4
Preparation for academic life	119	70.8
U.S. life/cultural/history	117	69.6
Establishing cross-cultural relationships	114	68.0
English language proficiency requirements	112	66.7
Local transportation	110	65.5
Community participation	103	61.3
Library tours	97	57.7
Shopping	87	51.8
Academic skills training	58	34.5
Intake interview	55	32.7
Leadership participation	37	22.0
Other (party, dinner, social activities, taxes traffic safety, counseling, geographical)	42	25.0

[a]168 questionnaires (one did not answer these questions)

primarily concerned with administrative and/or legal matters.

Respondents then identified the teaching techniques and presentation modes of their orientation programs (see Table 3). Three programs used lectures only; one used only discussion. More typically, programs combined discussion sessions, lectures, and question-answer formats. Slightly more than half used excursions and field trips and/or films, videos, or tapes. All the other methods, most experiential, were employed in less than a third of the programs surveyed. The "other" category included the use of foreign student handbooks and handouts, individual advising, one-to-one interviews, and various social activities.

Program Development:
The Role of Theory, Research, and Evaluations

How are orientation programs developed and improved? With what theoretical concepts are practitioners familiar, and which do they actually apply?

TABLE 3

TEACHING TECHNIQUES/MODES OF PRESENTATION

Techniques/Modes	No. of Programs	% of Totals[a]
Question-and-answer	149	89.8
Discussion sessions	135	81.3
Lectures	135	81.3
Excursions/field trips	91	54.8
Films/videos/tapes	86	51.8
Small-group projects	46	27.1
Experiences/case studies	43	25.9
Simulation exercises	31	18.1
Intercultural workshop	29	17.5
Other (foreign student handbook, handouts, individual advisement, social activities)	28	16.9

[a]166 questionnaires (three institutions did not answer this question)

Familiarity with and application of theoretical concepts are shown in Table 4. Of the 154 who answered the question about theoretical concepts, 18.8 percent said they were familiar with some of them but applied none. Culture shock was by far the most familiar concept and the one most applied. Across all the concepts, the application rate was only slightly more than 50 percent. Overall, then, practitioners appear to apply only half the concepts with which they are familiar.

Slightly less than half (46.7%) of the 169 practitioners said they use some form of research or evaluations in formulating their orientation programs. The rest (53.5%) said they do not. Of those who do, 59.2 percent listed books, newsletters, and other publications as their sources: most were familiar with publications by leading theorists in the field or by large international organizations. Only one practitioner listed an unpublished master's thesis among materials used. For program development and improvement, more than a quarter of the respondents rely on their own evaluative studies. Only a few use models developed by other institutions (5.6%), their own informal experience (4.8%), or their own studies or materials (2.4%).

About three-quarters of the respondents reported that they evaluate their programs; of these, more than half evaluate the programs individually, about a third said evaluation is periodic, and 19.2 percent said it is annual. Most—81.6 percent—use evaluative judgments by the orientation program staff, and 66.4 percent use participant questionnaires. Other evaluation means include long-term follow-ups (16%) and faculty questionnaires (14.4%), academic measurements such as GPA (8.8%), and such miscellaneous methods as personal contact and discussions with the students (5.6%).

TABLE 4

THEORETICAL CONCEPTS

Concept	No. and % familiar with it[a]		Application by those familiar with it		Overall application rate
Culture shock	147	95.5	116	78.9	75.3
Assimilation/adaptation	126	81.8	74	58.7	48.1
Reentry shock	124	80.5	61	49.2	39.6
Ethnocentrism	122	79.2	65	53.3	42.2
Multicultural person	114	74.0	52	45.6	33.8
Culture-general/-specific	109	70.8	71	65.1	46.1
Public/private self	92	59.7	42	45.7	27.3
U- and W-curve	75	48.7	54	72.0	35.1
Halo effect	72	46.8	18	25.0	11.7
Third culture	72	46.8	22	30.6	14.3
Cognitive shift	65	42.2	25	38.5	16.2
Attribution theory	61	39.6	21	34.4	13.6
Emic/etic	50	32.5	11	22.0	7.1
High-/low-context culture	46	29.9	22	47.8	14.3
Subjective culture	43	27.9	20	46.5	13.0
Trait/situation distinction	34	22.1	10	29.4	6.5

[a]Fifteen respondents did not answer this question at all. Of the 154 who did, 29 stated that they were familiar with at least one of the concepts but did not apply any.

9

TABLE 5

WHEN PROGRAMS BEGAN

Decade	%
Unknown	14.6
1940s	1.3
1950s	7.6
1960s	15.8
1970s	34.2
1980–85	26.6

"Appropriateness of contents to meet objectives" was the evaluation standard of 96 percent of the practitioners. "Students' satisfaction" was used by 91.2 percent, and 63.2 percent were interested in "the appropriateness of modes of presentation for multicultural audiences."

Finally, we asked several questions about the institutional context of orientation programs that reflect strongly on their development. As Table 5 shows, most—about a third—were first organized by colleges in the seventies.

Only about a fifth (19.8%) of the institutions have established regular courses for credit designed for the continuing orientation of international students. These take the form of orientation classes (28.3%), intercultural communication (23.3%), U.S. culture (23.3%), teaching assistant courses (6.7%), U.S. economics (3.3%), and several "other" subjects (15%) such as history, educational psychology, advanced language study, expository writing, action anthropology, cross-cultural counseling, and an intercultural communication course open to all students.

How well are the goals of orientation programs known and understood by top administrators, teaching faculty, and the international students and faculty themselves? Almost all the respondents answered this question. Sixty-two percent said their top administrators do, 14 percent said they do not. About a third said their teaching faculty do, a third said theirs do not, and a third said they were not sure. Sixty-five percent said their international students and faculty know and understand their goals; only 11 percent said they do not. From these data it seems that teaching faculty most need education about the purpose of orientation programs.

Problems and Suggestions

Of the 169 responding practitioners, 119 of them listed 246 problems and 150 suggestions. The problems were summarized in seven categories and the suggestions in four categories (see Table 6).

10

TABLE 6

PROBLEMS AND SUGGESTIONS

Subject	Problems		Suggestions	
	no.	%	no.	%
Time	60	24.4		
International students	54	22.0		
Institutional support	50	20.3	13	8.7
Funding	30	12.2	16	10.7
Outside resources	22	9.0	35	23.3
Programming	18	7.3	86	57.3
Miscellaneous	12	4.9		
TOTAL	246		150	

NOTE: 119 of the 169 respondents answered this question.

Time. Nearly a quarter of the problems related to time: the amount available for the program itself, staff time, and scheduling. Causes included late and varied student arrival and conflicts with other campus orientation and registration activities, resulting in staff overload. One practitioner said, "If we have [orientation] several days before registration, when we have time and staff to do it, we have a low attendance rate; if we have it immediately preceding registration, attendance is better, but we can't spare the staff time to do it properly; and if we wait until after registration, we can't do the administrative things that must be done before enrollment." None of the suggestions dealt directly with this problem, although some funding issues referred to it indirectly: that more funding could provide more staff and thus more time (in staff hours available).

International students. Almost a quarter of the problems were seen as "inherent" in the clientele. These include differences among international students (academic backgrounds, cultures, English proficiency and sophistication, interests and goals, religions, financial resources, and travel experience) and in their perceptions and motivation (which concentrate on immediate needs such as housing and registration). Upon arrival they may be suffering from fatigue, homesickness, disorientation, loneliness, and general anxiety, all of which interfere with the learning process. Practitioners complained that students do not participate actively, ask questions, or prepare for sessions; that they do not see it as important, take it seriously, or attend all the segments. Some nationality groups resist attending orientation at all. Some students mistake the international student advisers' office for the Immigration Service. All these factors make it difficult to plan programs for group size, content, sophistication, and so forth. One

11

practitioner summarized the problems by saying that "the ones who need orientation don't come." Again, there were no suggestions that dealt directly with this problem.

Institutional support. Twenty percent of the problems related to perceived lack of support from other offices, academic departments, and school administrators. Practitioners complained of a lack of communication and understanding about program content as well as the importance of student participation. Some accused their faculties of provincialism and their administrators of institutional apathy. The main complaints about administration were a failure to make orientation compulsory, to schedule it for integration with general orientation, and to open housing facilities early enough for international students to arrive in time to participate. The respondents believe this is due, at least in part, to general lack of understanding of the special needs of international students, compared with those of U.S. students. The 8.7 percent of suggestions that referred to this area included putting international student orientation on the school calendar, making it mandatory, emphasizing it in admission letters to international students sent from other offices, publishing an international newsletter to improve communication, involving various university personnel in the programs, and inviting key personnel to a social gathering.

Funding. Twelve percent of the problems listed focused on funds for program materials, program development (in length and content), and more staff. (However, many financial problems were "hidden" in other problem areas, such as time and programming.) Close to 11 percent of the suggestions related to this problem, most of these being ideas of what to do if more money were available. There were not many suggestions on how to obtain more funding. Participant fees are thought to lower attendance. One institution assesses each student an orientation fee, and the international student office gets a percentage based on the number of graduate and undergraduate students participating in their program.

Outside resources. Nine percent of the problems pertained to the involvement of presenters and helpers from outside the international student office: bankers, health care personnel, insurance and housing staff, departmental faculty, U.S. students, and "veteran" international students. The problems stemmed from these participants' lack of cross-cultural awareness (cognitively lumping international students into one homogenous group), their motivation, and complications of scheduling (at difficult times in the academic year). Almost a quarter of the suggestions (23.3%) addressed this problem, but they focused more on what might be done with different groups of outside resources than with how to motivate them to participate at all. Suggestions included using international and U.S. students as tutors and facilitators for small-group work in cross-cultural communication, as orientation aides, and as presenters about student life in the United States; using veteran international students as assistants to bridge the gap between new students and advisers; training students to work individually with new students; providing a support group of community homestay programs; engaging more "professional time" (such as a professional psychologist for counseling) in the orientation programs; networking "everybody from the president of the university to the mayor of the city" during program planning; and, most importantly, training outside helpers cross-culturally.

Programming. Only 7.3 percent of the listed problems related to programming: what and how much to do, and how and when to do it. Content problems include identifying international students' special problems and determining program priorities, the degree of individualization needed, and whether to include culture-general materials. Programmers also want to cover enough topics in sufficient detail without risking "information overload." Method problems involve finding the right mix of informational and experiential learning, and the best means of delivery. Timing problems involve placing the program effectively in the student's arrival experience, as well as the sequencing of program components. Some miscellaneous programming problems listed were whether to offer orientation for credit, combine it with ESL testing, or establish an on-going, full-time, all-year program.

More than half—57.3 percent—of all the suggestions related to programming. Most definitely, the practitioners favored ongoing or at least extended orientation rather than one-time programs upon arrival. They argued that students can not absorb more than very practical information at the beginning, and that many problems do not develop or are not perceived until after a month or two. They suggested orientation retreats off-campus, mainstreaming orientation for early contact with U.S. students, housing all international students in one dormitory during orientation, providing more prearrival information, and providing an intensive, pre-orientation live-in situation. Most of them desired better, more diverse materials such as films, videos, and computer programs. They wanted to use more experiential, informal, or athletic methods.

As for content, many suggestions focused on integration in the community and learning how to function effectively in American society. One practitioner said, "It would be a good idea to cut down content information in orientation programs and instead focus on the process of adapting to a new environment and upon informational resources." Others favored following students' perceived needs in determining content through a needs assessment or advisory board of international students.

13

Miscellaneous. Fewer than 5 percent of the listed problems fit into none of the above categories. They included practitioners being new to the field, not knowing where to find concrete information, and not being whole-heartedly convinced of their "mission."

Summary and Conclusion

The data collected in this survey cannot be called representative: only 169 out of 600 practitioners answered it, and most of their surveys were incomplete. Many wrote that they found it too comprehensive and time-consuming. Nevertheless, the results are revealing and useful.

Clearly, orientation practice is mainly concerned with registration, visa and Immigration Service information, and academic and administrative rules and regulations. The methods and techniques employed are geared to speed. But the problems and suggestions described by the practitioners show they feel that "real" orientation should be more, and that there is a continuum of what orientation can accomplish. This continuum ranges from "nuts and bolts" information to meet immediate needs, to "culture specific" issues about the United States, to "culture general" principles of intercultural communication. It is the last two areas that practitioners feel are neglected in most existing programs.

A combination of the practitioners' suggestions provides a picture of an ideal orientation program:

1. It should be an ongoing process that deals with students' problems as they emerge, beginning with survival information, continuing with cultural issues about life in the United States, and then, ideally, with culture-general topics such as "cultural awareness."
2. It should be centrally organized by one office, drawing on many resources across the university to offer the best possible information and help in each content area.
3. It should be integrated into the university calendar as a legitimate and important part of the academic year.

It is troubling that no suggestions were made to directly address the two biggest perceived problems (time and the international students themselves), while the most suggestions were made about an area that presents the least problems: programming. But judging from their many suggestions about programming, practitioners think that better programming will win more support, more funding, and thus more staff time and program length. They also feel that more interesting and relevant programs will lead to higher attendance rates and eventually reduce international students' problems in the long run.

The low application rate of theoretical concepts raises a question for the theorists and researchers who have introduced them: have the concepts been operationalized well enough to lend them readily to practice? On the other hand, practitioners do apply concepts in their practice, consciously or not. One wrote, "It is very hard to determine the influence these theories/concepts have on practice. I believe the incorporation of such concepts is more subtle and unconscious." Therefore, we might question the responses of the 18.8 percent who said they were familiar with one or more of the concepts listed but did not apply any of them.

Obviously, there is no such thing as "the" orientation program for international students. Practitioners are not unanimous about content or method. Conditions at institutions are different, and so are the actual programs. Though this is sometimes confusing, it is not necessarily a bad thing: practitioners need to be eclectic in their approaches and adapt what is available to their respective situations. The exchange of information between practitioners helps them do just that, and to find or develop new approaches that can be shared in turn. In a young, growing, relatively unstructured field like ours, this informal flow of information seems particularly important.

2

The Development of Preacademic Training Programs for Incoming Fulbright Grantees, 1951–1969

James E. O'Driscoll

Preacademic training for grantees arriving to study in the United States is a benefit that is provided to participants in the Fulbright program by the Division of Academic Programs of the United States Information Agency (USIA). It consists of programs ranging in length from a few weeks to an entire summer. Programs today all share the goal of helping incoming grantees adjust to life and study in the United States by providing them not only with needed academic skills, but also social and cultural skills. A major objective of the training, beyond its participant-generated objectives, is to create a group identity and to heighten grantees' awareness of the Fulbright program's goal to achieve long-range educational exchange purposes rather than to meet short-term policy goals.

In 1938, the U.S. Department of State established a Division for Cultural Relations, the first U.S. government agency specifically mandated to provide foreign nationals with opportunities to learn about the United States. Among the division's achievements was the institution in 1940 of the first U.S. government sponsorship of international student exchanges. Under its aegis, large numbers of grantees from Latin American republics came to the United States. The Institute of International Education (IIE) was requested to assume general administration of this program. IIE, which had been involved in educational exchanges since the 1920s, designed programs to ease participants' transition into life and study in the United States. Most of these programs had been on a small scale. Typically, incoming students were taken for a week of social interaction in Connecticut. As the numbers of grantees increased, the designers of preacademic training programs faced new challenges. A week in the country could hardly be expected to meet the needs of students whose level of English language proficiency was low. Increasingly, the responsibility for meeting the orientation needs of incoming grantees was shifted to their host institutions.

These first government exchange programs contributed to an increasing awareness on campuses of the need to provide a wider range of services to foreign students. The Department of State requested IIE to convene a meeting of key persons responsible for advising foreign students. In 1942 the first Conference of Foreign Student Advisers was held in Cleveland. A number of the issues raised clustered around preacademic training. There were only three year-round and eleven summer institutes in the entire country teaching English to foreigners who intended to pursue academic studies in the United States.[1]

The second major influence on the development of preacademic training programs for Fulbright grantees was the Department of the Army's Grants in Aid and Relief in Occupied Areas (GARIOA) program. GARIOA was designed for students from Germany, Austria, Japan, and the Ryukyu Islands to "re-orient" future leaders of countries that had recently been defeated in World War II. For our purposes, the greatest interest of this program lies in its concern for cultural issues and behavioral patterns, and its belief that an essential purpose of the grant was the orientation of the recipient.

In 1949, the first year in which the Fulbright program was fully operational, IIE placed 350 Fulbright and 200 GARIOA grantees at U.S. institutions. The designers of both fellowship programs assumed careful screening of candidates for language proficiency prior to selection. Thus, administrators believed that a mass didactic orientation at the port of entry would adequately meet the grantees' needs. It became apparent, however, that language training was needed, at least for some of the Japanese. For the cohort of over 850 GARIOA grantees in 1950, the Department of the Army established ten orientation centers on campuses throughout the country.

The general scheme executed in 1950 was judged successful. The next year the Department of State joined the Department of the Army to sponsor a planning conference for programs that would include Fulbrighters. The Conference of Orientation Center Directors, known as the Chicago Conference, met in March 1951. It marked the start of the development of preacademic training for incoming Fulbright grantees. Two documents from the Chicago Conference bear close examination. One was a Draft Memorandum of a proposed statement of purpose and guidelines for planning and implementing orientation programs for incoming Japanese and Ryukyan GARIOA grantees. The other document was the Revised Statement produced as a result of the conference to guide implementation of programs for both Fulbright and GARIOA grantees.

The Draft Memorandum enumerates six goals for the proposed programs. The fourth goal gives a fair example of the style and content:

17

> It is hoped that the Japanese will be emotionally and sentimental-
> ly drawn to us; that they will like us and trust us enough as indi-
> viduals and as a people to give a spiritual drive to their demo-
> cratic aspirations; that their hearts will join their minds in a
> genuine urge to cooperate, learn and share.[2]

Interestingly, there is no mention of English language needs, in spite of the
fact that the original impetus for establishing the program in 1950 was the
language deficiency of some of the GARIOA grantees.

The opening speaker at the Chicago Conference restated the objectives of the summer program thusly:

1. To bring the level of English comprehension and expression to the
   conversational level as quickly as possible;
2. To begin the interchange of ideas, the interplay of varying international experiences, and the examination and discussion of the "whys"
   (and how important they are) and the "hows" of American life, as
   soon as possible.[3]

The Revised Statement, designed to guide directors in implementing
summer programs, was issued later in the spring. It said summer programs
for incoming Fulbright and GARIOA grantees should:

1. Enable the student to increase his English language proficiency in
   order that he may undertake academic work in the United States
   without serious handicap;
2. Increase the student's knowledge of the general principles and events
   which have contributed to the growth of modern American Civilization, and enable him to observe, first-hand, the practical application
   of the principles of democracy to American life and institutions;
3. Accustom the student to American classroom techniques, and ac-
   quaint him with the general workings of the American educational
   system;
4. Afford an opportunity for the student to become acclimated and adjusted to a new social environment.[4]

In general, the Revised Statement is more relaxed than the Draft
Memorandum and leaves room for greater scheduling discretion on the
part of program directors.

In summer 1951, a total of 959 Fulbright and GARIOA grantees attended orientation programs on 20 campuses across the United States. All
were language programs with a strong admixture of orientation to U.S.
academic, social, and cultural life. Participants in summer programs were
usually sent to campuses other than the ones where they would spend the
academic year. It was felt that doing so offered the grantees a broader
experience of the United States and the variety of its academic life; also,

isolation from their academic institutions encouraged participants to concentrate on the activities of the orientation program rather than to anticipate their academic programs.

Each center received a broad mix of nationalities to encourage a wide-ranging exchange of ideas and experience, an early appreciation of the worldwide interactive nature of the Fulbright program. Half of the program activities were reserved for language instruction. The guidelines clearly assumed that social- and cultural-orientation content was not deliberately incorporated into language instruction: one had language, or one had orientation. There was concern that some aspects of the program design might be, or had been interpreted as, propaganda. However, by and large, the 1951 summer program was judged a success. On this basis the Department of State invited IIE to implement a similar program in 1952 for incoming Fulbrighters.

The orientation center directors met again to plan the 1952 orientation program. Its goals for incoming Fulbright grantees were:

- To give the student a feeling of being able to cope with the daily problems of living in the United States. The most important aspects of this are

  1. Fluency in English;
  2. Familiarity with the general workings of the American Educational System; and
  3. Knowledge of the most important social customs of the American People.

- To place before the student the major aspects of American Culture in such a way that through reading, observation and discussion he will come to a general idea of the historical forces which motivate the people of the United States...

- To give the government-sponsored student an understanding of the purpose and method of operation of the program under which he has come to the United States...

- To discover the student's own motivation in coming to the United States and to fix the possible limits to the accomplishments of his purpose in the light of facilities available and the purpose of the program.[5]

The chief goal of preacademic training had become "to put the foreign student on a fair competitive basis with his American fellow students."[6] A major consideration in so restating the objectives was to ensure that the summer programs were not interpreted as either propaganda or indoctrination.

This evolution of the statement of objectives should be seen in the larger context of the debate about the goals of the Fulbright program as a whole. In the late 1940s and early 1950s, this debate was held on a world stage. It began with an attack published in *l'Humanité*, which called the Fulbright program the intellectual phase of Marshall Plan imperialism. In spite of such attacks, or perhaps because of the clarification of purpose that they occasioned, the program actually gained wider acceptance. Johnson and Colligan (1965) believe that this acceptance overseas was in proportion to the degree to which it was perceived to be free of propaganda.

No sooner had the directors gone home from the 1952 planning conference than returns from an IIE survey began to pour in. A questionnaire had been sent out to student participants in the 1951 program, but the results had not been anticipated as necessary for the 1952 planning conference. To explore further the issues raised by these unexpected negative comments, a one-day conference for grantees in the Northeast was held in New York in April. As a result of student suggestions, program variations were introduced in 1952 to better meet student needs. Language instruction was de-emphasized. A further innovation was the use of homestays arranged by the Experiment in International Living.

By summer 1953 the GARIOA had been phased out, partially absorbed into the Fulbright programs for the countries involved. As a result, the total number of students for summer orientation programs declined slightly, and the number of orientation centers was reduced to eleven. The differentiation of program design from center to center continued: some were designed to receive primarily the language proficient, and others were designed more for those in need of additional language training. Directors were allowed greater discretion in implementing general program design.

In the next years, a number of changes were incorporated into the programs as they developed. Nineteen fifty-four saw the establishment of the first regional center—for grantees from the Far East, at the University of Hawaii. To a degree, the regional center concept opposed the multinational intent of the earlier objectives, and it was later phased out. In the late fifties, the preacademic training centers were urged to incorporate homestays into their programming. In 1956, recommendations were made to include foreign students on the staffs of programs, and to establish programs even more closely focused on particular fields. Although field-of-study programming had been suggested by student participants as early as 1952, a narrow focus of academic orientation was specifically excluded in previous programs, presumably because it seemed incompatible with the goal of creating a broad base of intellectual exchange across national and disciplinary boundaries.

In the first five years of the training programs, a major transformation in perception of the program had occurred:

1. An activity that had been seen very briefly in the light of short-term policy promotion was now seen as an activity with long-range

cultural and social bridge-building purposes through its support of educational exchange.

2. Preacademic training, which had been seen as a self-contained activity fulfilling its goals in six weeks, was now viewed as an ancillary activity in support of the objectives of the overall Fulbright program.
3. A program that had originally been constructed to suit exclusively the ideas of its organizers had learned how to adapt itself to the felt need of the student participants.

The next period in the history of the preacademic training program focused more on development of the program design than on program philosophy. It was not until 1960 that rather obvious changes were made to deal with two persistent problems: late arrivals, and the range of language ability among the grantees. Designers of the 1960 program decided to vary program length to better meet the needs of grantees. Those in need of language instruction were assigned to eight-week programs with the assumption that after a certain amount of intensive support in English as a second language (ESL) training an academic orientation could be phased into the program. Four-week programs were established for those at a higher level of language proficiency but with little familiarity with U.S. life and its academic system. Two-week programs were designed for those grantees who could be expected to have greater familiarity with the United States.

Almost as soon as the system was in place, it had to be modified. Greater demands were placed on the preacademic training program by two factors: a combination of increasing numbers of grantees with a relatively low level of English language proficiency, and a greater awareness on the part of universities that language proficiency is an element to be considered in academic admission. In response to this trend, grantees began to be placed in regularly scheduled campus ESL programs prior to their participation in the Fulbright preacademic training programs.

In 1963, the Department of State encouraged regularly scheduled ESL programs to include academic, cultural, and social orientation components. It provided subsidies for non-sponsored students attending programs that included such a component. This program so encouraged the spread of the orientation concept that by 1974 it was hard to imagine an ESL program on a U.S. campus that did not combine language instruction with orientation.

In 1969 a major cut in the Fulbright program's funding affected its planning and implementation. A 40 percent drop in the number of participants accelerated a trend in the sixties: the movement away from total reliance on contract centers toward utilization of a limited number of regularly scheduled, university-administered programs. In addition, a change in the nature of the student participants became apparent. Incoming grantees were now on the average more widely traveled and better informed about the United States and the world than earlier grantees had been. They were better prepared academically for their study in the United States. They were more aggressive, resourceful, and willing to use critical judgment. This resulted from changes in world communication and from increased selectivity of the nomination process due to the decrease in the number of grants offered.

Budget cuts in 1976 further reduced preacademic training for Fulbright grantees. Only grantees in serious need of ESL instruction were assigned to summer programs. By this point, fewer than ten percent of incoming Fulbright grantees participated in preacademic training. Most grantees proceeded from their home countries directly to their academic institutions. For the first time, lack of language proficiency was made the sole criterion for assignment. Almost immediately a reaction began. Posts in some countries expressed concern about their candidates' increased levels of anxiety. Officers within USIA pressed to restore preacademic training programs for countries whose candidates were generally proficient in English. In 1978, academic, social, and cultural orientation for black South African Fulbright grantees was restored. In 1980, recognizing that language deficiency—however important—was not the single cause of maladjustment to U.S. academic life, USIA requested IIE to restore the three-week programs of academic, social, and cultural orientation.

In 1983, USIA made a major policy change to be consistent with this trend. It broadened criteria for assignment to once again allow virtually all eligible grantees to receive assignments to preacademic training. The three-week programs of academic, social, and cultural orientation were strengthened. One of the major objectives of the change was to restore the sense of community among Fulbright grantees and thus strengthen their identification with the goals of the program.

USIA, IIE, and the administrators of programs that have received Fulbright grantees are currently involved in an evaluation study of the participants' orientation needs and of their perceptions of the benefits they have received from orientation programs. The results of this study will shape the planning and implementation of future Fulbright preacademic training programs as they evolve.

Endnotes

1. Institute of International Education, Report of the Conference of College and University Administrators, April 29th–30th and May 1st, 1946. IIE, New York.

2. IIE, Draft memorandum as a basis of discussion, 12 December, 1950. An unpublished document in the files of IIE's Office of English and Special Services, 1–2.

3. Revised statement—orientation program 1951 in IIE's *Foreign Student Orientation Program.* IIE, New York, 1952, 7.

4. Ibid., 13.

5. *Foreign Student Orientation Program—July 28–September 5, 1952.* Unpublished document in the files of IIE's Office of English and Special Services, 4–5.

6. Ibid., 5.

References

Unpublished Material*

Hoover, Lyman, ed. 1952. Proceedings, evaluation conference for students from other countries.

Institute of International Education. 1951. Foreign student orientation program.

_____. 1951. Report on the foreign student orientation program—1951.

_____. 1952. Foreign student orientation program: July 28–September 5, 1952.

_____, (Orientation Division). 1953. Review of reports on orientation from foreign students who attended orientation centers, summer of 1953.

_____, (Foreign Student Department). 1954. Report on orientation program, July–September, 1954.

_____. 1955. Orientation program report, summer 1955.

_____, (Department for U.S. Exchange Relations). 1956–60. Orientation program reports.

_____, (Foreign Student Department). 1961, 1962. Orientation program reports.

_____. 1969. Orientation programs, final report, 1963–69.

_____, (Division of Special Courses). 1970–73. Final reports, orientation program.

_____, (Orientation and Enrichment Programs). 1974, 1976. Orientation program, final reports.

_____, 1976. 1976 summer English language program, final report.

_____, _____. 1978. Reports of English language training, summer 1977, 1978.

_____, (Office of English and Special Services). 1979–82. Reports on preacademic training for IIE-related grantees.

_____. 1983, 1984. Reports on preacademic training for USIA-related grantees.

_____. 1950. Draft memorandum as a basis of discussion, 12 December, 1950.

Center Director's Meeting. Minutes. December 12–13, 1968.

Orientation Center Directors' Meeting. Minutes. April 13–14, 1971.

(Also consulted were files for Center Directors' Meetings held in 1963, 1964, 1967, 1968, 1971, 1973, 1974 and 1975, as well as reports of summer programs submitted beginning in 1959 by academic institutions that either had special contract arrangements or received concentrations of Fulbright grantees for preacademic training.)

*In the files of IIE, Office of English and Special Services.

Published Material

Halpern, Stephen Mark. 1969. The Institute of International Education: A history. Doctoral thesis submitted to the Faculty of Political Science, Columbia University.

Institute of International Education. 1938–1983. Annual reports.

_____. 1946. *Report of the Conference of College and University Administrators and Foreign Student Advisers*. New York: IIE.

_____. 1942. *Report of the Conference of Foreign Student Advisors*. New York: IIE.

Johnson, Walter and Francis J. Colligan. 1965. *The Fulbright program: A history*. Chicago: The University of Chicago Press.

Keeffe, Emily C. and Elizabeth Converse. 1952. *The Japanese leaders program of the Department of the Army. An evaluative report*. New York: IIE.

3

Brief Course on America: An Orientation to the Study of American Culture

Harvey Sarles

Each summer since 1980 the author has taught a ten-day course to about 75 incoming Fulbright graduate scholars. It is a course that attempts to portray American culture as Americans live and understand it. It is intended for the visitor who finds the study of America interesting or important and wants to go about seeing who Americans really are.

As I teach this course, I imagine a dialogue between the teacher and newly arrived non-Americans who will spend a year here pursuing their studies, living with and among Americans. I approach it as an anthropologist who has lived abroad for three years and has had the opportunity to look back at America through the experience of other cultures and the constant translations of their languages. The course is an ongoing attempt to sense the exotic within the ordinary of everyday life in America.

Setting the Stage: The American Mythic Ideal

One of the course's goals is to communicate to the students the collective myths of American culture, which provide a key for interpreting Americans' complex and often contradictory behavior. Roughly, I describe them as the myths of opportunity, providence, and individualism.

Whatever the wonders or difficulties of everyday life, Americans retain some collective sense that their country is a place of great opportunity. Having come here from other places, our ancestors abandoned their respective histories to become Americans. Deep in our mentality there is a sense of America that John Adams described in 1765: "the opening of a grand design and scene in Providence for the illumination of the ignorant, and the emancipation of the slavish part of mankind all over the earth" (Jones 1960, 5). Here everyone can do and be whatever his or her desires and abilities merit, with cleverness and hard work. This, at least, is the myth that continues to inspire us, and the myth by which we seem to judge and treat the rest of the world. History, therefore, is our American history. We have a sense of the brief present, but only a small sense that much of the rest of the world is very deeply invested in and bounded by its own histories, and of what that might mean.

Secondly, Americans are always at work trying to create "providence," a progressive idea of a perfect world. At the same time we have a deep compassion, believing that everyone on earth should be able to partake in this providence. In his book *On Excellence*, John Gardner (1961) points out that our twin ideas of excellence and egalitarianism are always in tension. The providence myth demands that we be the "best"; the emancipation of the world demands that we be open to everyone equally.

The underside of the providence myth is that when we perceive a lack of progress, we are confused about the meaning of our lives and our being. We cast in various directions to find a reason and to search for new inspiration toward the America we can idealize. Thus our ideal of collective providence apparently carries within it an anti-ideal, an evil or satanic element that we invoke to account for dilemmas. Historically, we have blamed other countries (for example, the Soviet Union, new immigrants, minorities, the rich, the poor, the "immoral"). We have used these anti-ideals to help us regather our national pride and sense of unity as Americans. Our constant truth has been that the world is ultimately changeable, and that with proper conditions and leadership we can "get back on track" toward our providential role in the world.

Finally, there is the myth of individualism. In America, inspiration, education, and social policy seem to work best when they concentrate on individual growth and development. Most successful plans in America offer personal "incentives" that are perceived to benefit each individual rather than any "classes" of types of persons; the latter are usually considered "welfare" plans meant to maintain, rather than to "uplift" or "educate," their recipients. Individualism, linked with our personal virtue, dominates our judgments and valuations, if not our actuality. We seem to "work hard," sometimes purposefully and other times because work itself is virtuous.

These myths provide a frame of reference for the topics the course will explore. The topics themselves have emerged over the years into the following arrangement:

Day One: Geography
Day Two: Government, Part I
Day Three: Government, Part II
Day Four: Population and Roots
Day Five: Class, Religion, and Ethnicity
Day Six: The Media and the Market Economy
Day Seven: The Religious Right

Day Eight: American Foreign Policy
Day Nine: A Folk Chronology
Day Ten: Remaining Problems

The topics progress from the concrete to the more abstract, from how America is structured to how it actually works. This topical progression is natural and effective. For example, discussion of the religious right is placed at the low energy point of the course, where it renews the students' interest and the intensity of their discussion.

Day One: Geography

The students have arrived already full of impressions, assessments, and stereotypes of America, so on the first day I begin with a neutral topic and a large political-relief map of the United States. The map provides a continuous visual impression and an opportunity to practice thinking of and speaking the English names and places. We start by locating and discussing Minneapolis and St. Paul; then we talk about distance and travel time, and they begin to feel the vastness of the country. We discuss why particular cities came to be located where they are, and how transportation and communications function across the continent.

Day Two: Government, Part I

We read the Declaration of Independence and begin the Constitution. I talk about what they represent to help draw the students out of their more temporal perspectives. These documents remind them of America's peculiar history, beginning with a revolution that continues to live in many Americans' minds. In the Declaration of Independence I point out the particular derivations from the French Enlightenment, including the parallel notions of egalitarianism and individual excellence.

Reading the Constitution, we discuss the concept of "checks and balances." Inevitably the students inquire about the political parties and the executive's power. Here I venture ahead with a discussion on how television and the market economy enhance the president's power to affect journalists. As we consider "who is a citizen," we preview discussions about American Indians and slavery. The subject of the Supreme Court triggers questions about law enforcement, police, the nature of law, the underground economy, and the military. The president's "commander in chief" political control over the military is of special interest to students who strike comparisons with their own countries.

Day Three: Government, Part II

Today we begin with a discussion of the executive branch of the federal government. Describing the cabinet provides insights into our government's concerns. The departments of State and Defense draw the most interest from these students, who have applied for visas from our embassies and whose governments are affected daily by U.S. foreign policy. They ask how ambassadors are appointed, how embassy staff is trained, and how our military is organized. They are also curious about competition, and about freedom of movement between the states.

We move on to the constitutional amendments. The Bill of Rights, especially the First Amendment, takes time. I mention the American Civil Liberties Union, and I provide history on our universities' academic freedom (Metzger 1955). We move on to religion and discuss our idea of church/state separation, which amazes students from countries with state churches. The thirteenth through fifteenth amendments remind the students how recently we abandoned slavery, and we talk about how race relations remain a troubling problem. Another absorbing issue is prohibition and how societies regulate drugs and other substances. Finally we look at another relatively recent law, universal suffrage, and discuss the women's movement in the United States, the Equal Rights Amendment, and several related issues: family life, changing attitudes, women's work, family care, and divorce.

Day Four: Population and Roots

I set the stage today with a description of this continent before the coming of the Europeans. I talk about the many Indian peoples, languages, cultures, and philosophies. I contrast this with the Indians' experience since the Europeans came, and with their Hollywood image from which these students have derived most of their perceptions. We consider an urban Indian slum a mile from the university; the Bureau of Indian Affairs; and Wounded Knee. I describe the Indians' historical conceptual inability to put a cash value on land, as well as the current success of a few Indian groups.

The students in this class, I then suggest, are a metaphor of who is American today. This idea clashes with America's portrayal abroad as substantially middle-majority white. America does orient itself toward its English roots, demonstrated most clearly by its language. But through history, most people—white and non-white—have come here to escape poverty, many to attain religious freedom.

America's immigration, slow with occasional bursts, is still evidenced in the ethnicity of many of our cities. This vast pluralism seems held together by a "glue" of surprising integrity: a sense of what it means to be an American despite many differences. It perplexes students who come from countries where people have lived in the same place since antiquity. We discuss how immigration—cutting people off from their histories—has seemed to allow the United States to avoid some of the regionalism or tribalism that continues to plague many nations.

Another strong feature of the American people has been an "entrepreneurial-individual spirit." The class considers how this has affected who got into which businesses. One example is the itinerant Jewish peddlers who followed the frontier and eventually founded the great dry goods and department stores across the country. Another is the WASPish (we pause to define "WASP") control of most corporations. We examine the American process by which the most recent immigrants enter the economy in menial jobs, then become educated, save money, and move "up" into Middle America within a generation or two. Exceptions are Indians, who never immigrated; blacks, most of whom immigrated against their will; and Hispanics, who more than any other group have retained their own language. These three remain a relatively permanent "underclass" in America (Auletta 1982).

Day Five: Class, Religion, and Ethnicity

Today's discussion expands on yesterday's topics of population and roots. America becomes very complex, almost unbelievable, to many of the students whose societies are clearly class-distinguished according to royalty, aristocracy, great wealth, etc. I immediately point out that most social relations here are negotiable and without clear rules. The students have already experienced our informality and inconsistent use of titles.

America's social classes, I suggest, are a product of our fortunate geography, vast resources, and entrepreneurial spirit. The students see evidence in the plethora of goods and food everywhere, which seems to some an excess. Since World War II our "middle class" has done well, especially in terms of its expectations. The great poverty that does exist is less related to a "lower class" than to where people have settled in relation to opportunities, and how recently. The "really rich" are, with a few exceptions, essentially private and hidden in homes fringing urban areas.

Another surprise—despite our peculiar church-state separation—is the religion/social-class relationship. We survey America's myriad religions, from relatively upper-class Episcopal (derived from the Anglican Church) to the relatively lower-class urban Catholic and fundamentalist Southern Baptist. Class lines are blurred within the denominations, however. For example, Italian-Sicilians have become educated and successful enough by now to gain "placeness" in the once predominantly Irish Catholic church. Also, since World War II Jews have moved into the religious mainstream and are no longer considered a minority. We discuss how, also since World War II, many ethnic and religious restrictions on jobs and positions have been broken down. I encourage the students to try to enter at least some of these religious and ethnic social structures to gain perspectives and perhaps penetrate American thinking.

We close this day with a bridge to tomorrow's topic by discussing social class as material wealth—cars, single family dwellings, schools, social mobility, and the expectation of choice. Are these standards changing, we ask. And why are there poor people in this rich America?

Day Six: The Media and the Market Economy

Many Fulbright fellows in the past several years have expressed a sense of tragicomedy that an actor could be president. This becomes their metaphor of America as a market economy: we elect a president just as we buy a product advertised on television.

We discuss the changes television has brought to America, particularly in the political arena. It has also affected our social lives: Americans have probably narrowed their outlooks as well as their circles of acquaintances and interactions because of television. The students are already appalled at the lack and poor quality of international news they have found. I raise the issue of news selection according to television's need to be exciting and brief and the networks' need for high ratings. I bring in the weekly Nielsen ratings and explain how they translate into advertising dollars. We explore whether television's pace tends to shorten and rework our sense of national and global history. I recommend "Nightline" and "The MacNeil-Lehrer Report" as the best available television reportage.

The students are curious about news gathering and selection for print media, too. I recommend the best papers for international coverage, and suggest they look at the weekly news magazines as examples of what many Americans see and read.

Day Seven: The Religious Right

No survey of current America would be accurate without an examination of the "religious right" and its impact on American politics and society. Today I use elements particularly from our Day Three discussion of the Constitution's church/state separation. I preface the discussion also by identifying my long involvement with this issue as it affects academic freedom in a state-supported university.

There are usually many non-Christian students to whom this is all new, so I begin with a historical view of the Old and New Testaments. To approach fundamentalist Christianity I introduce "scientific creationism" (Morris 1974), basically an interpretation of the Old Testament's Book of Genesis through a New Testament orientation. I define this fundamentalism as a literal exegesis of specific biblical texts (e.g., a six-day creation). Scientific creationists hold that all ideas, including modern science, rest on beliefs or assumptions; they have thus gained an apparent equivalent status of religious creationism with modern science. Here I stress the power of the idea of "fairness" to Americans (Nelkin 1977), how we hold apparent opposites as equivalent and feel compelled to hear both sides.

Modern science strives to be open to retesting and rethinking based on observation. Creationism rests on biblical texts attributed to a God who cannot be mistaken. I introduce the concepts of "secular humanism," absolute morality, and "original sin." Throughout the discussion I quote from Henry Morris, a major intellectual of the scientific creationist movement, tracing the roots of his work to Plato's *Phaedo* and the New Testament. We discuss fundamentalism's effect on education and its tendency to undermine the Constitution's implicit "rule of law," and we speculate on its adoption as a state religion.

But why has Christian fundamentalism emerged as such a powerful political force today? We consider the strong fundamentalist faction within Islam, which has arisen as a reaction against the perceived loss of morals and culture in the face of Western "development," technology, and materialistic values. Christian fundamentalism reacts against the drug culture, divorce, economic depression, uncertainty, a growing "intellectual nihilism" among humanists, and a sense of America's failure or weakness. To explain our failed destiny as a Paradise-on-Earth, we too seek a Great Satan to blame.

Day Eight: American Foreign Policy

In 1984 Nicholas Hayes, a Soviet intellectual historian and professor, accepted my invitation to lead a class discussion on American foreign policy. His perspective lent credence to the treatment of this complex and critical subject. Hayes began this discussion by marking the birth of modern American foreign policy at the end of World War II. That war defined most of our dominant issues, including the Cold War and U.S. rearmament.

First, the very experience of World War II differed dramatically between the United States and the U.S.S.R., which emerged from decades of church-supported royal despotism and a traumatic revolution only to sustain horrifying losses on its own soil. A vast number of maimed people over age fifty are still painfully visible there today. America, on the other hand, emerged from a devastating depression to go abroad and deliver the world from a clearly evil enemy, Hitler's Germany.

Hayes pointed out America's early and persistent tendency toward isolationism (articulated in George Washington's warning against foreign alliances) and our sense of virtue. These two factors, he suggested, have pushed us into positions where we perceive ourselves alone but also responsible for others' moral health. Then in World War II we were

31

powerfully propagandized to distinguish issues as black and white. Our use of the atomic bomb to end the war in 1945, for example, was considered a merciful necessity and a relief. Emerging dominant from the war accentuated this tendency to simplify. We began to depict the U.S.S.R., especially Stalin, as the inheritor of the evil Nazi character; the U.S.S.R., acting on its more painful history, tended to act in ways that confirmed our worst fears. Thus, the war has continued—sometimes vague, sometimes very real—between America and its enemy, World Communism.

Hayes attributed the inner-directedness of our foreign policy to the experience of our rulers. Having matured at the end of World War II, they have always known America as the strongest and wealthiest world power; thus, America's position is perceived as natural rather than cyclical, to be defended and preserved more than studied or understood. Hayes also cited our vastness and relative isolation globally as a contributing problem: Americans must go a very long way to speak another language (except Spanish), and our international travel habits also insulate us. We have little appreciation for other peoples' experiences or histories, and both individually and as a nation we react to them on our own terms.

In conclusion Hayes touched on some continuing problems in our foreign policy: the murky issue of world debt, our potentially explosive policy toward the Third World, and the paradox of a world economic-political order at odds with our continuing tendency toward isolationism.

Day Nine: A Folk Chronology

Nearing the course's end, we now develop a "folk chronology" to help integrate the diverse topics we have covered. This chronology is a history of the current population's life experience, so I begin by reviewing America's demographics: the low Depression population, the postwar "baby boom," the drop in birth rate after 1963, and another rise since 1975. Our population in general is aging, which presents important problems to be solved.

Our folk chronology begins with the Depression, still vivid in older Americans' memories. We discuss labor and unions, the powerful National Labor Relations Act, and why socialism and communism have done poorly here. World War II affected people now in their fifties with a strong sense of community involvement and clear vision. Our postwar power, our idea of providential America, and our identification of communism as evil pushed us abroad and into the Cold War. The Korean War was a very different experience, without clear winners or losers. World War II veterans garnered love, respect, and heroism never awarded to vets of Korea and, later, Vietnam.

Technology's impact became profound in the fifties, and it has continued. Both television and computers have "privatized" American life. In 1957 Americans watched the Soviets launch Sputnik, and for the first time we began to sense an international technical challenge beyond the arms race. The challenge, along with our baby-boom young adults, made us feel the sky was the limit. The optimism carried our economy to the early seventies.

The sixties saw dramatic change. It was a decade of enfranchising minorities—blacks, the handicapped, and women. We moved from brinkmanship with the Soviets at the Bay of Pigs to staving off the "domino effect" in Southeast Asia. Surplus baby-boomers in a booming economy now turned to new drugs and became hippies and flower children, activists and demonstrators. Tragedy entered with the assassination of our first Catholic president, the charismatic John Kennedy, in November 1963—a black marker in many Americans' memories. It continued with riots and protests through the assassinations of Robert Kennedy and Martin Luther King, Jr., in 1968. President Lyndon Johnson's pursuit of both civil rights changes and victory in Vietnam produced great turmoil. On the one hand, general opinion toward blacks, and blacks' sense that change toward equity was possible, turned an ugly period into one of perceived progress. On the other hand, disillusionment with the war was devastating.

The early seventies saw our bitter exit from Vietnam, which seemed to many a major defeat for American culture. Compounded by Nixon and Watergate, it came to represent the time when America lost direction, moral purpose, and hope. On top of this struggle, the OPEC cartel imposed a four- to five-fold increase of our fuel prices. With war debts and a shrinking youth population, our once-carefree economy turned bleak. We found we had become careless competitors in the global marketplace, and that we had fallen out of favor with many countries. The Carter administration did not interpret the world in a way that was palatable or simple. The gloom of the late seventies set the stage for Ronald Reagan's optimism.

I then backtrack to pick up a fundamental thread in the story: the women's liberation movement. The movement clarified and gathered momentum in 1973, when the Supreme Court ruled that women had a constitutional right to obtain abortions. More and more women were working outside the home, and the divorce rate was rapidly increasing. Fundamental change in male-female relationships created a new style of life for many if not most Americans, redefining living arrangements and marriage. The confusion surrounding roles, expectations, and responsibilities has produced strong reactions, including impetus for the religious right, especially against abortion. It has also allowed impressive gains for women in the workplace and politics, symbolized powerfully by Geraldine Ferraro's nomination for vice president on the Democrat ticket in 1984.

Day Ten: Remaining Problems

On the last day we critique the course and talk about some of the issues the students find especially puzzling or problematic. Divorce is very troublesome. We consider its many possible causes: industrialization, urbanization, migration, mobility, the loss of extended family support, a weakened sense of community, and the women's movement. Another contributing factor may be what Lasch (1979) called "narcissism," a concern with individual development and freedom. Since the early sixties in America, there has also been a shift away from organized religion toward psychotherapeutic explanations for individual and family problems. The students again see reasons why fundamentalism and criticism of our institutions have become so powerful.

Secondly, even after the explanations provided in this course, many students cannot believe how little Americans know or think about their foreign policy and the rest of the world. I review the psychology of immigration, and we peruse the map of America again, discussing its vastness and relative isolation. Most Americans, I suggest, seem not so concerned with other places, but with trying to find the America that we all desire.

This is only a bare introduction to the study of America, I conclude. I tell the students that Americans need to study, but that we also need their criticism. It is their task to study us and to understand us well, so they can analyze us in our own terms as well as theirs.

References

Auletta, Ken. 1982. *The underclass.* New York: Vintage Books.

Gardner, John W. 1961. *On excellence, can we be equal and excellent too?* New York: Harper & Row.

Jones, Maldwyn A. 1960. *American immigration.* Chicago: University of Chicago Press.

Lasch, Christopher. 1979. *The culture of narcissism.* New York: Norton.

Metzger, Walter P. 1955. *Academic freedom in the age of the university.* New York: Columbia University Press.

Morris, Henry M. 1974. *Scientific creationism.* San Diego, CA: Creation-Life Publishers.

Nelkin, Dorothy. 1977. *Science textbook controversies and the politics of equal time.* Cambridge, MA: MIT Press.

4

Foreign Student Orientation at the University of Pennsylvania

Ann Kuhlman

At the University of Pennsylvania the foreign student population, totaling more than 2000, consists primarily of graduate students (80%) representing almost 100 countries. This population is about 75 percent male and 50 percent Asian, with heavy academic concentration in the fields of business, architecture, and engineering. Each September the university welcomes about 550 new students, 100 scholars, and 200 dependents. The Office of International Programs (OIP), which is institutionally responsible for foreign students and scholars, operates under many of the same constraints faced by similar offices in other universities and colleges—understaffed, underbudgeted, and primarily oriented toward problem management rather than program development.

Programs, services, and academic requirements, as well as orientation activities, differ among the university's twelve graduate schools. While the university offers an extensive orientation program for new undergraduate students, it offers nothing comparable for new graduate students. That task is left primarily to the individual graduate schools and departments, with a small number of activities sponsored by the university's Office of Student Life. Therefore, some new foreign students find the Office of International Programs one among many sources for information, clarification, and support; for other students it is one of only a few resources they have. OIP's orientation program is thus designed to meet the widest set of concerns and issues in an effort to ensure that new foreign students, regardless of their academic affiliation, have equal access to information and service.

OIP's orientation for foreign students, like that of many other institutions, begins with carefully prepared prearrival information sent well in advance of the student's departure for the United States. The materials include detailed practical information and suggestions for the best way to prepare for the cultural and sometimes educational adjustments that lie ahead. A tentative orientation schedule is included, and new students are encouraged to visit OIP upon their arrival. This mailing not only provides important information to help answer questions and reduce anxieties, but also acquaints the student with the supportive role OIP plays for foreign students. Experience shows that this kind of communication prior to arrival guarantees a high rate of participation in the orientation program.

By mid-August the final preparations for the fall orientation program are underway. In order to handle the increased workload during the orientation period, a graduate student intern, two student employees, and about 20 student volunteers are added to the foreign student advising staff. The orientation packets are assembled and the program schedule set. The office reception area is rearranged to accommodate the increase in traffic, and the closet is cleared for storing baggage. The emergency loan fund is in order, and efforts made to insure a minimum of initial financial problems. Colleagues in the university and friends in the community are alerted to possible special needs. The city is scouted for affordable temporary housing.

The fall orientation program is held between September 1—when on-campus graduate housing becomes available—and the first day of classes, usually the Thursday after Labor Day. Activities are scheduled to conflict as little as possible with the new-student activities of the graduate schools. OIP staff plan and schedule the program in conjunction with other service and administrative units involved with graduate student orientation, such as the Office of Student Life, Graduate Residences, Graduate Student Government, and the International House. While no one office professes to have a complete graduate-student orientation program, cooperation between these offices in jointly-sponsored activities has led to a greatly expanded program. This cooperation has also provided more opportunity for foreign and American students to meet one another outside the departmental/ school context. In addition, it has greatly expanded the resources available to OIP in terms of developing and supporting orientation activities.

The objectives of OIP's orientation program may be outlined as follows:

- to provide students with the practical information that will enable them to cope with the immediate needs of settling into a new environment;
- to familiarize students with the main features of their new cultural, educational, and social environments;
- to offer students the opportunity to socialize with faculty, staff, and other students;
- to extend a warm and personal welcome from the University of Pennsylvania.

The current orientation program has evolved over the years through many successes and failures. The main features of the program include passport registration, personal orientation, and a more general group orientation. OIP has moved away from long information sessions that included presentations on a number of topics to a combination of more specialized presentations, more extensive written information, and a more personalized welcome.

A new student first registers with OIP by presenting his or her passport. OIP offers a brief explanation of the relevant immigration regulations and then gives the student an orientation packet. The packet includes an extensive handbook that not only addresses immediate concerns but also serves as a reference for semesters to come. It also includes information about health care and insurance, university facilities and resources, safe living, and transportation systems, to name a few. Student volunteers, U.S. and foreign, have provided a more individualized welcome for each new student. While the new student waits to talk with a foreign student adviser, the student volunteer goes through the packet, highlighting information on housing, health insurance, course registration, and the logistics of getting around campus and the city.

This personalized approach has proven highly successful both for the new students, providing them the opportunity to ask questions and meet an "old hand," and for the OIP staff, who now have more time to handle the more problematic cases. We also encourage members of the various nationality groups to be available to new students. Several of these groups provide OIP with lists of students who can be called upon to help. This kind of assistance is invaluable because it gives attention that OIP staff cannot always provide.

Long information sessions have been replaced with a shorter and slightly more formal "Welcome Assembly." This program, attended by approximately 60 percent (300) of the new foreign students, serves as the official welcome to the university (usually made by a representative of the central administration) and gives OIP staff a more structured occasion to introduce themselves and a number of their colleagues in the student service division. Unlike OIP's longer information sessions, which tended to result in "information overload," the Welcome Assembly allows us to remind students of the more critical and immediate matters. Speeches and remarks are kept to a minimum, and the mood is relaxed. A lively reception, attended by a number of faculty and staff, follows the presentation.

In addition to the Welcome Assembly, the orientation program includes the following activities:

Academic Life Workshop. A three-hour workshop on U.S. graduate education with presentations by students, teaching assistants, and faculty, this workshop conveys information about the academic system and promotes discussion of the student's and the institution's expectations. The University of Iowa's videotape on graduate student life helps initiate this dialogue.

Safer Living Workshop. OIP, Public Safety, and Off-Campus Living staffs present information on how to live safely and securely in an urban environment.

Orientation Program for Spouses and Families. This informal two-hour program designed by the International Women's Group in cooperation with the International Programs and University graduate residences introduces spouses to the services and programs, to the staff of the various offices, and to one another.

Getting to Know Americans. A panel of five veteran foreign students talk about their experiences in meeting and making friends with Americans and their own techniques for overcoming "culture shock."

Introductory Tours. Campus, library, University Museum, International House, and city tours are conducted, most often led by student volunteers. International Classroom program staff host the University Museum tour, giving them an opportunity to introduce their program. The International House tour also provides its staff an opportunity to explain its programs and services, including the host family program and English language classes. (This information was previously conveyed in an information session rather than "on site.")

Social Activities. One of the important objectives of OIP's orientation program is to give new students the chance to meet their student colleagues, new and returning, U.S. and foreign. The orientation program is supplemented by a number of social programs: OIP open house, social hours, volleyball games, an all-afternoon Labor Day barbecue, and an international student party. In preparing for these activities we most effectively combine our efforts with other offices and organizations involved in the orientation.

OIP's "success" with the orientation program can be attributed to several factors: well-developed written materials; effective use of student volunteers; use of non-traditional hours and flexible scheduling (such as scheduling activities in the evenings and over Labor Day weekend); and cooperative programming efforts with university and community organizations (showing that you don't have to "do it alone"). OIP's program is by no means definitive, but has improved continuously. In the past years OIP has initiated a number of activities and has developed a well-balanced program that effectively meets the needs of most new foreign graduate students at the university. The number of students participating in the program has increased notably. OIP has relied and will continue to rely upon their feedback to further improve the program's format and content.

5

Orientation Services for A.I.D.-Sponsored Participants in Programs Administered by Partners for International Education and Training

Judith A. Cadman

For more than three decades, the U.S. Agency for International Development (A.I.D.) has supported the training of nationals from developing countries through visitation programs in the United States. These programs have three objectives: (1) to develop local staff for A.I.D.-assisted projects, (2) to strengthen public and private institutions, and (3) to develop local training capabilities. Virtually all program participants are currently handled by contractors and/or programming agents. More than 200 contractors perform a range of participant training activities. According to A.I.D., the number of participants in these activities increased from 6,000 in FY 1978 to more than 18,000 in 1988.

One of A.I.D.'s principal programming agents is Partners for International Education and Training (PIET), a consortium of four private, non-profit organizations: the Asia Foundation (San Francisco), the African-American Institute (New York), AMIDEAST (Washington, D.C.), and the Experiment in International Living (Brattleboro, Vermont). Each institution possesses expert knowledge of a specific region of the world. Approximately 4,200 participants are processed annually on all A.I.D.-related academic programs, specialized technical courses, or study observation tours. They are monitored by the staff in PIET's central office located in Washington, D.C. and in each of the four consortium members' headquarters. Programs administered by each of the four regional offices usually include one or more of the following six orientation phases: *Predeparture Orientation*, provided by the A.I.D. mission's overseas representative in the home country; *PIET Orientation*, an administrative briefing conducted by a PIET staff person soon after a participant's arrival in the United States; *Arrival Orientation*, on U.S. culture and survival skills, conducted during a participant's first week in the United States by the Washington International Center; *Ongoing Orientation*, on U.S. and local culture and survival skills, provided by academic and training institutions; *Enrichment Seminars*, provided by independent agencies; and, finally, *Reentry Orientation*, offered by independent agencies and some academic institutions.

Orientation for most participants begins with a predeparture briefing consisting of a review of logistical information provided by a mission training officer (usually a host-country national). The quality of the orientation depends to a large extent on the creativity of that officer, the time available for him to conduct it, and the quality of briefing materials. Since the majority of missions do not send participants in large groups, orientation programs are usually conducted on an individual basis. They focus almost exclusively on administrative issues, to the exclusion of those related to cultural adjustment (Cadman 1984a).

Whenever possible, participants are programmed to visit one of the four PIET regional offices or the central office for their administrative briefing immediately upon their arrival in the United States. The following general topics are covered in all briefings: (1) how PIET functions; (2) general responsibilities of PIET participants; (3) visa information; (4) budget details (allowances, per diem); (5) insurance coverage; (6) plan of study; (7) details for travel to training institutions and for international travel; (8) the importance of the exit interview; (9) professional development opportunities; and (10) life in the United States (Foust 1984).

Most PIET long-term academic participants then attend a six-day comprehensive orientation program offered by the Washington International Center (WIC) in Washington, D.C. As described by its former director, Robert Kohls, WIC is the oldest institute of its kind in the United States. It was founded as the "Democracy in Action" program in 1950 by the American Council on Education at the request of the U.S. government. Its founding purpose was to provide orientation and hospitality for foreign dignitaries coming to the United States from Germany, Japan, and Austria. Today, WIC is a program of Meridian House International, a nonprofit cultural and educational institution dedicated to enhancing international cooperation and understanding. Meridian House International is under contract to A.I.D. to provide cultural orientation programs to participants (*U.S.A.I.D. Handbook X* 1981).

According to WIC program director Carol Watt, "The goal of the new WIC orientation program 'Discover the United States' is to encourage international visitors to develop skills that will allow them to be independently effective in a new culture" (Cadman 1988). WIC's program objectives are twofold: (1) to introduce participants to various aspects of U.S. culture and society, and (2) to ease participants' adjustment to living and studying in the United States, minimizing "culture shock" that might interfere with their training. Multilingual intercultural trainers and lecturers explore with participants both theoretical and practical information about the United States, including social behavior and cultural values, the political system, pluralism and multiethnic groups, male-female relationships, and adjustment strategies (Washington International Center 1987a). Sessions deal with intercultural communication and cross-cultural relations between U.S. and non-U.S. societies [and] help participants recognize cultural differences in American approaches to decision-making and interpersonal relations (Cadman 1984b).

WIC uses a participatory approach to intercultural training and orientation. This enables the international visitor to take an active role in understanding the underlying forces that shape American political and cultural behavior. The six-day program begins with a needs assessment of the visitor that provides staff with an opportunity to make modifications in the program; this is followed by a series of lectures/discussions and moves toward more experiential activities. The training sessions emphasize the developmental changes in behavior that will facilitate adjustment to U.S. culture (Washington International Center 1987a). As a complement to in-house seminars and discussions, field trips provide visitors an opportunity to interact with the community. Historical tours, cultural programs, professional contacts, and home hospitality are other significant parts of the program (Washington International Center 1987b). The orientation program has a wealth of practical cultural material designed to be used as independent information or to augment the main program. The material is presented in a series of booklets that provides visitors, especially those preparing to study at U.S. universities, with information too detailed to be covered during campus orientations (McCaig 1988).

Ongoing orientation is provided by academic and technical training institutions for academic participants. PIET recognizes that campus services and orientation programs that include community programs and activities may vary in quality and comprehensiveness. Continuous communication and collaboration between PIET's monitoring staff and the international student advisers and academic counselors are important for the provision of adequate ongoing orientation.

Enrichment seminars fill a special professional (as opposed to cultural) need for many participants in academic programs; they provide an important complement and significant contribution to the U.S. training experience. (PIET does not usually provide supplemental training activities for the participants in technical programs because these programs are shorter and more tightly scheduled.) Some training groups that provide enrichment activities include the Management Training and Development Institute (formerly Management Communications Associates), the Agency for International Development/National Council for International Visitors, and mid-winter seminars and professional conferences related to field of study.

The Management Training and Development Institute's seminars expose participants to communication principles fundamental to management. Often the A.I.D. participant coming to the United States for academic or technical training returns home to a job that requires new management responsibilities. A regular component of these seminars is the preparation of the participants for reentry into their own culture (Cadman 1984c).

Mid-winter seminars sponsored by A.I.D. and the National Council for International Visitors (NCIV) comprise another of the enrichment programs offered participants. Each December, A.I.D. sponsors cultural and social programs of approximately ten days in length throughout the United States. The programs are organized by local international visitors centers and coordinated by NCIV (Seidel 1984). NCIV, like WIC, is under the umbrella of Meridian House International. These seminars occur during the Christmas vacation. They include lectures, discussions, workshops, field trips, and home stays (Cadman 1984d). "The objective of the Mid-winter Community program is to provide A.I.D.-sponsored participants with diversified educational, social and cultural experiences which enable the participant to understand better the U.S. and its people as a society in continuous development" (*U.S.A.I.D. Handbook X* 1981).

The sixth and final phase in the orientation process is reentry. At the conclusion of an intensive stay in the United States, participants must reintegrate to their own cultures in order to successfully transfer their newly learned technological skills. The only reentry orientation presently offered to PIET participants is implemented by the international student offices, university campuses, or Management Training and Development Institute seminars. Through small group discussions, simulations, and case studies drawn from personal experiences, some participants explore the fundamental issues of "reentry." For the majority of participants, however, participation in an exit interview and/or a formal evaluation of their training program is the norm.

Evaluation

Hired through the Bureau of Programs and Policy Coordination, consultants Laurel Elmer and Tom Moser reviewed 206 evaluation studies and related reports of A.I.D.-sponsored projects spanning a period of 30 years in all geographic regions in which A.I.D. has operated. Cadman (1984e) reports that 141 of the total number of reports evaluated made general recommendations; of these, 72 reports contained 244 recommendations related specifically to orientation (approximately 1,400 recommendations were recorded in 12 categories; orientation was the category receiving the highest ranking). The findings also indicate that the demand for better and increased orientation services has been consistently made throughout the entire 30 years of A.I.D. project activities.

It is clear from the literature review of A.I.D.-sponsored training programs that orientation has been viewed as a critical component of any training intitiative throughout the entire 30 years of training described in the report. Improved technical and academic training programs must, by definition, include improved and expanded orientation services in order to maximize the impact of the training process and the ultimate success of the transfer of technology.

References

Cadman, Judith. 1984a, October. Interviews with Leila Mogannam and Elizabeth A. Carter, regional coordinators for Near East/Asia and Africa/Latin America, respectively; Bureau of Science and Technology (A.I.D.), Office of International Training.

_____, 1984b, October. Interview with Dr. Robert Kohls, former executive director of the Washington International Center, Meridian House, Washington, D.C.

_____, 1984c, October. Interview with Dr. Robert Morris, director, and Ms. Ginni Cook, former assistant director, Management Communication Seminars (now MTDI).

_____, 1984d, October. Interview with Mr. Phil Uncapher, former director of training, Mid-Winter Seminars.

_____, 1984e, October. Interview with Laurel Elmer, independent consultant, U.S.A.I.D., and coauthor with Thomas Moser of *Review of Participants Training Evaluation Studies Report*.

_____, 1988, March. Interview with Carol Watt, program director, Washington International Center, Meridian House, Washington, D.C.

Elmer, Laurel and Thomas Moser. 1984. *Review of Participant Training Evaluation Studies Report*. Washington, D.C.: U.S. Agency for International Development, Center for Development Information and Evaluation, Bureau for Program and Policy Coordination.

Foust, Stephan. 1984. PIET Organization Outline. Unpublished raw data.

McCaig, Norma M. 1988. WIC Resources: The *U.S.A. in Brief* Series. *AMIDEAST Advising Quarterly* 1(4).

Seidel, R., ed. 1984, September. *Operations Manual: Placement, Programming, Management of A.I.D. Participants*. Contract No. PDC-10030-C-002207-00. Washington, D.C.: Partners for International Education and Training.

U.S.A.I.D. Handbook X Participant Training. 1981, April. Washington, D.C.: S&T/IT.

Those interviewed for each section:

1. Mission Predeparture Orientation

   Elizabeth A. Carter, regional coordinator for Latin America and Africa
   Leila Mogannam, former regional coordinator for the Near East and Asia
   Office of International Training
   Bureau of Science and Technology

2. Washington International Center

   Robert L. Kohls, former executive director
   Carol Watt, program director

3. Mid-Winter Seminars

   Phil Uncapher, former director of training

4. Management-Communication

   Robert Morris, director
   Ginni Davis-Cooke, former assistant director

5. Partners for International Education and Training

   Ronald E. Springwater, executive director

Additional information came from the following sources:

1. *U.S.A.I.D. Handbook X*, April 1981.

   Handbook X provides the policies, regulations, procedures, and guidance on A.I.D. participant training for use by personnel of A.I.D., other federal agencies, contractors, universities, and other organizations who have responsibilities for, or contribute to the training of, A.I.D. participants. It applies to all participants who receive training under A.I.D. funding or sponsorship.

   —Handbook X, Chapter 11, 1-1

2. *PIET Operations Manual*, November 1964.

3. *PIET Brochure*, 1983.

4. Office of International Training, A.I.D.

5. Regional Office Orientation Outlines, PIET:
   The African-American Institute
   The Asia Foundation
   The Experiment in International Living
   AMIDEAST

6. Washington International Center. 1984. *Brochure*.

   _____. 1987a. *Discover the United States (statement of purpose)*.

   _____. 1987b. *Why should you let us welcome and orient your international visitors to the United States*.

6

Cross-Cultural Half-Way Houses: Orientation within Intensive English Programs

Patricia Byrd

Over the years, intensive English programs have both narrowed and broadened our understanding of what it means to "teach English." They have narrowed it in that we now are trying to teach the specific kinds of English needed to achieve particular goals—the English of science and technology, the English of the academic world, and so on. They have broadened our vision as we realized that, in helping people to learn to use English, we must also help them to understand and participate in U.S. culture. The cross-cultural orientation activities of intensive English programs grow out of the programs' structure and out of the cross-cultural problems created by this unique set of purposes, methods, students, faculty, and administrators.

Barrett in his "Introduction" to NAFSA's *Administration of Intensive English Programs* (1984) outlined the defining characteristics of such programs. In sum: (1) Traditionally, intensive English programs have been offered by institutions of higher learning (of course, numerous privately operated intensive English programs of high quality exist, and academic affiliation is no guarantee of high standards); (2) intensive English programs have year-round sessions, usually following the academic calendar of their parent institution; (3) they have at least three levels—beginning, intermediate, and advanced; (4) standardized testing is used for placement and evaluation of English proficiency; (5) students are adults who have at least a high school education and are planning to enter academic programs in the United States; (6) students are in class a minimum of 20 hours per week (additional hours of planned activities, including field trips and conversation classes, are available); (7) the chief administrator of the program has at least an M.A. in teaching English as a second language (TESL) or linguistics along with teaching and administrative experience (the teaching is done by a core of full-time teachers with degrees in TESL, linguistics, or

45

related fields—a varying number of part-time teachers are used); (8) students come from a wide variety of cultural backgrounds (a program can easily have students from 25–30 different countries); (9) different materials and methods are used for the different proficiency levels (the basic program is planned around the four language skills—reading, writing, listening, and speaking); (10) academic advising and personal and cultural counseling are available.

In short, an intensive English program is a full-time language-teaching program for adult, college-bound students from all over the world.

Students enter intensive English programs because they have limited ability to use English. In a 1984 survey conducted by the Regents Publishing Company, nearly 75 percent of the 1500 English as a second language (ESL) teachers who responded taught beginning-level courses. In the author's own experience, a typical intensive English program has a pyramid shape—a huge base of students at the beginner or low intermediate levels, a smaller group of intermediates, and an even smaller group of high intermediates or advanced students.

This high percentage of students with low English proficiency has two implications for the program. First, limited knowledge of a language almost automatically means limited knowledge of the culture in which the language is used. Second, it is extremely difficult to communicate even restricted information, much less the complexities of cultural understanding and adjustment. Thus, students who enter the program at this level are severely limited in their ability to understand what is going on around them and to learn quickly to deal with their new lives. Many who study in the United States are unsophisticated about even their own countries and cultures. Some countries' idealistic plans to incorporate lower levels of society into higher education lead them to send students abroad who would have had trouble living in their own capital city, much less the United States.

The limited English proficiency and frequently limited sophistication of the students makes the intensive English program their first place of contact with the United States. The program stands at a point between their home cultures and the United States. While it is possible to picture the intensive English program as a bridge between cultures, the image of a halfway house is more accurate. The purpose of the intensive English program is to help these sojourners learn to cope in a new world by providing instruction in new behaviors and a safe place in which to learn and make mistakes. Students enter the programs with very little skill at living in the United States; when they depart after a successful experience, they should be prepared for life outside the program's protective walls.

Achieving this goal is made more difficult by the inadequate training most ESL teachers have had in cross-cultural communication. The experience of living in another country and knowing that such living is difficult does not prepare a teacher to plan activities and programs that teach new skills to his or her students. Teachers in intensive English programs also experience culture shock. They spend their days with a fantastic mixture of cultures, few with which they can easily identify. The typical intensive English program classroom teacher is a woman in her mid- to late twenties with a master's in TESL or linguistics and some months of experience living in one country overseas. Even the most conservative of them are twentieth-century American women. Their typical students are males from Third World countries. The focus of "orientation" for intensive English program administrators and teachers will thus fix on students' relations with each other and with strange American females in class. Intensive English programs must also deal with stresses on the teachers, who must adjust to the students and create an environment in which language learning can occur.

Students and their sponsors add to this complex situation by a reasonable fear of indoctrination. Since the plan is for these students to return to their home countries, how much, they wonder, do they really need to know about the United States to function as students in the scientific and technical fields that most of them will choose?

The intensive English program must also deal with students who are narrowly focused in their understanding of the purpose of English instruction. To many students and sponsors, an intensive English program is really a preparation program for the Test of English As a Foreign Language (TOEFL). Anything else is considered by them a waste of time. Unsophisticated students and sponsors frequently will not see cultural training and orientation as a necessary part of language instruction.

An intensive English program usually has a very mixed student body. A typical class will have students from five or more countries. A truism of English teaching is that the more different languages the better, since it forces students to communicate in English as their common language. But think of such a class—four Cameroonians, three Venezuelans, two Saudis, one Japanese, one Chinese, one Iranian, and a Brazilian. The possibilities for communication are certainly abundant—and so are the possibilities for miscommunication. In truth, ESL students have as many problems dealing with the cultural strangeness of other foreigners as they do with that of Americans.

At the other extreme, but still an intensive English program possibility, is the single-language class—all Saudis, Venezuelans, or Japanese. Cultural misunderstanding can lurk in these classes, too. All Saudis are not from the same tribe or family or city; all Japanese do not come to the United States for the same purpose. A major difficulty for language and culture learning in such classes is that the U.S. teacher is a minority of one

47

within the class. The teacher's individual characteristics can be magnified to the status of fact about all Americans. The teacher is also more likely to feel an outsider and to have emotional problems of experiencing culture shock in his or her own country.

Both types of classes can suffer isolation from U.S. life even while in the United States because of the students' poor English. Naturally enough, they are reluctant to try to communicate in English when it is difficult to do so. It is also natural but regrettable that Americans are reluctant to interact with English-language students because such communication is difficult and restricted. Students in intensive English programs do not have much contact with Americans unless the program itself has taken steps to provide it.

Finding or developing useful materials is also very difficult. Publishers are only beginning to provide texts that address cultural topics, and texts not directly aimed at cultural orientation are also becoming more sensitive to cultural differences. Teachers are trying to include cultural topics for discussion and writing assignments. Unfortunately, the unsophisticated teacher can turn to impossible topics—compare your city to this city, or your country to the United States. A student who has been in a city only a few weeks cannot possibly know much about it, and his or her brief experience of the United States most likely will not lead to meaningful comparison with the home country. For that matter, the student probably has not thought analytically about the country.

Despite the foregoing problems, intensive English programs have several advantages in developing useful orientation programs. First is a captive audience. Students cannot decide that the orientation will be a waste of their time and refuse to attend when the orientation is cleverly mixed into the academic program. Also, unlike foreign student advisers who see students for limited numbers of hours each term, teachers in the program meet with the students for four to six hours each school day, with additional time on weekends for special events. Moreover, language teaching has to be about something—teachers do not teach pure syntax or abstract semantics, but willy-nilly include cultural content when they teach U.S. English.

Another advantage for teaching in intensive English programs is that the profession is in the first energetic stages of *becoming* a profession. Thus, teachers are willing to accept large amounts of training—and retraining—to meet newly understood goals. At the same time, scholars and researchers in the profession are very much interested in cultural matters, so that journals and conferences offer thoughtful discussions and recommendations.

In addressing their problems and taking advantage of their opportunities, intensive English program administrators and teachers have developed three approaches to cross-cultural orientation: introductory orientation sessions at the beginning of the term, classes on U.S. culture or cross-cultural communication, and cultural materials in regular classes focused on other topics or skills.

Like the larger parent institutions, the programs generally find it necessary to have some type of orientation at the beginning of each session. Some sessions deal strictly with survival information at this point, based on the idea that the students have too little English to benefit from wider-ranging orientation. Other sessions include cultural discussions as a way of introducing a topic that will be dealt with later in detail.

Many intensive English programs now include two types of classes that take cultural orientation as their basic purpose: those required of all students, and those offered as electives. While the model intensive English program for many years had a set curriculum that offered the students no choices, many current programs are experimenting with offering some selection to students, especially at the more advanced levels.

A class in reading quickly becomes a class in cultural issues because the reading materials cannot be cultureless. A class in writing must teach writing styles and formats of U.S. academic culture. Even a TOEFL preparation class deals with U.S. culture as the students learn to answer multiple-choice questions that are set in U.S. contexts.

Intensive English programs also have active extra-curricular programs of conversation groups and field trips designed for both entertainment value and cultural orientation. Field trips range from learning to take the bus on a shopping trip to attending sessions of Congress or visiting Disney World.

In conclusion, pioneering continues in U.S. intensive English programs—and not just in language-teaching methods and materials. Language teachers are of necessity also culture teachers. As organizers of classes and programs that bring together representatives of a variety of cultures—including themselves as representatives of the United States—these teachers urgently require the best possible ways to achieve cross-cultural understanding, or at least cross-cultural patience.

References

Barrett, Pat. 1984. Introduction. *The administration of intensive English programs.* Washington, D.C.: National Association for Foreign Student Affairs, 1–5.

Regents survey finds most ESL teachers well experienced. 1984. *TESOL Newsletter* XVIII, 4, August.

7

Training International Students
As Teaching Assistants

Mark Landa

The Teaching Assistant (TA) English Program at the University of Minnesota was developed to address a longstanding communication problem between some foreign teaching assistants and their students. Today, the program is providing instruction to 44 graduate students who are either currently holding or are expecting to hold TA appointments in their departments during study at the university.

The process of identifying trainees is a university-wide effort. At the beginning of each academic term, the assistant vice president for academic affairs and the dean of the Graduate School remind administrators of their responsibility to guarantee that those with teaching or advising duties "meet reasonable communication standards." Specifically, the administrators are expected to refer for proficiency testing those current or prospective TAs whose spoken English may be problematic. They are also expected to pay half the instructional cost of the classroom communication skills course for any of their program's or department's TAs required to take it.

The Minnesota English Center staff is then charged with assessing the proficiency of those TAs who are referred by the programs and departments and improving the proficiency of those TAs who do not meet an acceptable standard by providing them with an appropriate course of instruction.

Until now, the program's main instrument for assessing TAs' proficiency has been a test known as SPEAK, or Speaking Proficiency English Assessment Kit. There are seven sections in the test, each involving a particular speaking activity such as reading aloud, completing sentences, describing or narrating a picture or picture sequence, and reporting information. Each test produces an audiocassette of the examinee's responses. The responses are rated independently by two trained evaluators according to criteria established by the Educational Testing Service (ETS). Subscores for pronunciation, grammar, fluency, and overall comprehensibility are calculated. Recommendations are then based on the results.

The instructional component of the program consists of the course on classroom communication for teaching assistants and a more basic course for TAs who will need more than one quarter of training in English communication skills. The instructors are advanced graduate students in the Department of Linguistics and Program in English as a Second Language (ESL).

Class size is limited to nine. The courses meet for two hours once a week, and each student is given a one-hour individual tutorial each week. Total instructional time for each course participant is 30 hours.

The aims, materials, and instructional strategies emphasize skills and attitudes more than knowledge of language forms and structures. The course requires the TA to practice different types of presentational and interactional skills: for example, simulating the first day of class; defining a specialized term or concept in their subjects; fielding questions from students; explaining a diagram, model, or illustration on the blackboard. Presentations are videotaped and analyzed later in the tutorials. In brief, participants are introduced to an important skill, apply it in a classroom situation, receive feedback on their performance from peers and the instructor and through videotape, and identify areas of weakness for subsequent practice. Peer evaluation within the groups of nine and self-evaluation are an essential part in the process of developing better language, intercultural, and pedagogical skills.

Evaluation of the Minnesota TA Program

The program and course originated with complaints about the "TA problem" that go back many years. In the late seventies *The Minnesota Daily* printed several opinions, articles, cartoons, and letters to the editor about foreign TAs (*Minnesota Daily*, 29 September 1977 and 15 May 1978. Also 27 May 1983), some of which were xenophobic. In response, the ESL program extended its course offerings to include a course to improve the speaking skills of TAs. The course was offered as an option to graduate students, with financial support from the university's educational development program. Six students enrolled. Videotape was used on a limited basis. When the course was offered for the second and third times, it maintained its focus on interaction and presentation while greatly expanding the use of videotape feedback. The fourth time it was offered, the National Association for Foreign Student Affairs (NAFSA) provided a cooperative projects grant. At that time the course included three class sessions and a tutorial per week. The classroom work was divided into an ESL component and a cross-cultural teaching component (Mestenhauser et al. 1980). The course has since been offered during academic terms to approximately 220 students.

In 1982 the university's administration made a commitment to resolving the problem of poor communication by foreign TAs. A committee ap-

51

pointed by the university president recommended that a test of spoken English (administered by ETS) should be required of all non-native English speakers responsible for classroom instruction (Robinett 1982).

Enrollment in the course increased dramatically as an outcome of action by the Minnesota state legislature a year later:

> It is the intent of the Legislature that the University address the problem of teaching assistants for whom English is a second language. The University shall develop a plan for insuring that teaching assistants are proficient in speaking, reading, and writing the English language as it is spoken in the United States (Legislative Record, May 21, 1983).

The fact that the state government so explicitly expressed its concern made funding available for a much larger program than attempted previously.

From Basic Assumptions to Instructional Strategies

One assumption widely held in the university and the state of Minnesota is that the problem is caused by the TAs' language deficiencies. It has seemed obvious at first glance to undergraduate students, their parents, the TA supervisors, and department heads that communication problems stem from poor pronunciation, faulty grammar, and limited vocabulary. Students' complaints typically focus on the TAs' inarticulate or accented speech.

When TAs come to the course, they seem more prepared to accept a linguistic explanation of their reason for being there than one that derives from cultural differences. Some have assumed that they will become effective classroom teachers just by learning a sufficient number of new words, expressions, and grammatical structures, and by mastering their pronunciation. They seem to hold a learning model that has more to do with quantity and correctness than with communication.

Researchers and course instructors have found, not surprisingly, sufficient data to support this assumption (Shaw & Garate 1984). However, it does not follow from this evidence that the TA problem is exclusively or even primarily caused by language deficiencies, or that the solution lies only in language practice. Evidence of other, possibly even more serious, problems is beginning to accumulate.

Research at the University of Texas led to the conclusion that students' negative evaluations of their foreign TAs were more often based on social mythology than on linguistic reality (Orth 1982). Orth found relatively little agreement between undergraduate students and ESL teachers on the speaking proficiency ratings of foreign TAs. Undergraduates' ratings of teaching effectiveness correlated as strongly with student satisfaction and final grades as with speaking proficiency evaluations. In order of importance, student dissatisfaction with the TAs proved to be (1) inter-personal, (2) linguistic, and (3) intercultural. In other words, even if the TAs could speak perfect English, the foreign TA problem might very well exist. As one TA reported, she received both compliments and complaints on her English in the same class (*Minneapolis Star and Tribune*, June 6, 1983). Undergraduates probably react to many aspects of the TA's performance in their evaluations and judgments, but they consider "language problems" to be the only acceptable area in which to voice criticism.

Course instructors at many campuses have come to appreciate the crucial role that cross-cultural differences play in this problem. Shaw and Garate (1984, 28) have represented differences in expectations with unbal-anced equations in the relationships between U.S. students and foreign TAs. U.S. students have higher expectations of their professors and teach-ers than the TAs are able to satisfy, while the TAs expect higher academic capabilities than they experience from the U.S. students. Each side is disap-pointed in the other. Consequently, the course in classroom communica-tion at Minnesota and other comparable institutions, such as Stanford, the University of Southern California, and Arizona, have included either sepa-rate cross-cultural components or information and feedback on U.S. culture, values, expectations, and nonverbal behavior as they affect class-room interaction.

Other weaknesses noticed in foreign TAs' performance do not seem to have their causes in language and cultural differences. They have been noted also in American TAs and, indeed, among teachers everywhere: needless repetition resulting in boredom, running over time-limits, talking too fast or too slowly, lacking volume, inappropriate use of the black-board, illegible script, needless digressions, lack of organization and pur-pose, and poor judgments about what the students already know and need to learn. Because of the great range of linguistic, cultural, and pedagogical problems that may arise and the limited time available for resolving them, the success of the course depends on the full cooperation of the TAs and their commitment to modifying aspects of their behavior. Change in their attitudes is an even more critical underlying variable.

For TAs from certain cultural traditions, the change in their basic atti-tudes toward American culture is extremely difficult. Yeh (1973) has con-trasted the changes in attitude of Americans in Taiwan with the mainte-nance of Asian students' attitudes while studying in the United States: in short, the Americans looked forward to changing their views, while the Asians in general expected very little, if any, change. Given these expecta-tions, it may seem unlikely that a 30-hour course could have much of an im-pact. However, Yeh has also indicated that the student's life is primarily devoted to career development; the years are seen as an interim period essential to meet family obligations and acquire professional status and experience. The chance for students to adopt a broader cultural perspective, therefore, is much greater if the course in classroom communication skills can be closely tied to the concepts of career development and the acquisition of marketable skills.

For this sense of professional growth to result, academic departments must support the program philosophically as well as financially by placing value on classroom teaching as an essential part of career development. If those graduate students in a department who support themselves by teaching are looked down upon while those who do research are given more status, the important process of attitude change can be undermined. Being a TA must become viewed as more than a means of temporary self-support.

Observations of the TAs during the past six years have provided many indications of changes in attitude. No two TAs experience the process identically; in general, however, some stages in the process can be identified:

1. recognition of language deficiencies;
2. concern for improving communication with undergraduate students;
3. acceptance of feedback from videotape, course instructor, peers, and their own students;
4. willingness to consider cultural variables in classroom interaction;
5. realistic self-perception resulting in a balance of confidence and openness to change;
6. commitment to continued improvement.

Two underlying competencies that make learning all the classroom communication skills possible are the ability to monitor one's own "output" and the ability to modify it appropriately depending on the content of the message, the audience, and a range of linguistic, cultural, and pedagogical factors. The underlying competency is *not* correctness of language or perfect pronunciation (Stenson, Smith & Perry 1983). As the ultimate goal for most of the TAs, accentless speech would be unattainable in a period of ten weeks. In the meantime, given the right attitude, a set of compensatory skills *can* be acquired that will go further toward helping the foreign TAs gain acceptance from their students and achieve specific objectives in the broad areas of language, culture, and pedagogy.

Program Evaluation

A program that purports to change attitudes along with levels of skill attainment raises difficulties in evaluation. How does one measure attitude change? Is the course successful if skill improvement is not commensurate with changes in attitudes? Three sources of data have been gathered in a attempt to evaluate the program so far: (a) responses to questionnaires completed by the TAs themselves at the end of each course; (b) follow-up studies of individual TAs who have left the course and are assigned to classroom teaching; and (c) statistical data, including course completion percentages and comparisons of pre- and post-assessment results from SPEAK.

To evaluate the program from the perspective of TAs who complete the course, a standard form with ratings, rankings, and comments about specific course components is used. More useful than their global evaluation of the course, which has tended to be extremely favorable, is an attempt to identify the areas in which they felt they had improved the most. Not surprisingly, the area of pronunciation received the highest ratings during the year 1983–84. TAs indicated that they had gained not simply an awareness that there was a pronunciation problem, but some knowledge of the problem's nature and causes and how it might be remedied.

TAs also said that they had learned about cultural differences by using the *Manual for Foreign TAs* by Gary Althen, which has been required since its publication. By the end of the course, the TAs indicated a high level of self-perceived improvement in areas that involved the ability to adapt a presentation to an audience, learning what is expected of a TA, and nonverbal communication.

It is difficult to identify consensus in suggestions for course improvement. TAs' suggestions often derived from what they felt their own individual weaknesses or needs were:

- more use of American TA models
- more work on the basics of language
- more systematic study of grammar and pronunciation
- more intervention by the teacher
- more opportunities to have an audience for presentations
- better video equipment
- a more appropriate method of testing
- more closely geared to "my" major
- more time for presentations and tutorials

The TAs were somewhat divided in their evaluation of one particular assignment: observations of their departments' American TAs in the classroom. Only 20 percent felt the observations were helpful; 38 percent said they were not helpful, and the rest were unsure.

Follow-up Studies

We have claimed that the success of the course depends primarily upon its ability to change attitudes. In a case study follow-up of ten participants in the 1979–80 course, Landa and Perry (1984) conducted interviews with the TAs and their advisers and colleagues 12 to 18 weeks after the completion of the course. We intended to determine what difference, if any, the course had made in their teaching at the University of Minnesota, and in particular what aspect of the course had made the most difference. All of the TAs had continued to have language difficulties to varying degrees.

Five TAs in the followup had relatively successful profiles. They were aware of the factors inhibiting their successful communication with American undergraduate students but nevertheless choose to support themselves as classroom teachers. Through the TA course, they became aware of obstacles to communication and took steps to improve. They recognized their own need to develop techniques for interacting with American students who had never encountered a non-native speaker of English in the role of classroom teacher. Their self-evaluations were consistent with the external evaluations given through interviews with colleagues, supervisors, and students. They rated their own English skills as only good or fair, with the latter rating for pronunciation. They actively sought feedback from their students about communication in the classroom.

What factors had made the difference for the "successful" TAs? Although their language skills had improved, this study concluded that acquisition of the needed linguistic, cultural, and pedagogical skills depended primarily on the adoption of certain attitudes. To the extent that the course was able to nurture, to shape, or, in certain cases, to change the TAs' attitudes, it could influence their success or failure.

Conclusion

The TA English program has been put forth as the University of Minnesota's response to the legislature's requirement to address TA language deficiencies. While it has resulted in a viable process for monitoring and improving the TAs' skills, it has considerable room for improvement. Monitoring depends on the full support of all academic departments, but evidence indicates that not all TAs have been referred for assessment. As an assessment tool, SPEAK has proved to be at best a gross measurement of a limited number of speaking skills. Furthermore, the assumption that a one-quarter, 30-hour course for TAs will be sufficient may not prove valid. Finally, there is need for more objective evaluation of the course and more systematic followup studies of TAs who have completed the course.

References

Althen, Gary. 1981. *Manual for foreign teaching assistants.* Iowa City: Office of International Education and Services.

Landa, Mark and William Perry. 1984. An evaluation of a training course for foreign teaching assistants. In Kathleen Bailey, Frank Pialorsi and Jean Zukowski-Faust, eds., *Foreign teaching assistants in U.S. universities.* Washington, D.C.: NAFSA.

Mestenhauser, Josef et al. 1980. Report of a special course for foreign teaching assistants to improve their classroom effectiveness. Minneapolis: University of Minnesota International Student Adviser's Office and Program in English as a Second Language.

Minneapolis Star and Tribune, June 6, 1983.

Minnesota State Legislative Record, May 21, 1983.

Orth, John L. 1982. Attitude and native listeners' evaluation of speaking proficiency; the case of foreign teaching assistants. Ph.D. Dissertation, University of Texas, Austin, Texas.

Robinett, Betty et al. 1982. *International students at the University of Minnesota.* Unpublished manuscript.

Shaw, Peter and Elena Garate. 1984. Linguistic competence, communicative needs, and university pedagogy: Toward a framework for TA training. In K. Bailey, F. Pialorsi and J. Zukowski-Faust, eds., *Foreign teaching assistants in U.S. universities.* Washington, D.C.: NAFSA

Speaking Proficiency English Assessment Kit. 1982. Princeton, NJ: Educational Testing Service.

Stenson, Nancy, Janice Smith, and William Perry. 1983. Facilitating teacher growth: An approach to training and evaluation. *MinneTESOL Journal 3.*

Yeh, H. et al. 1973. The American student in Taiwan. *International Studies Quarterly* 17:359–370.

8

The Experiential Approach to International Student Orientation

Dario Gamboa

Traditional orientation programs for new international students at the University of Minnesota were similar to those for American students: lectures with practical hints on "what to do" and "what not to do," social events, and brochures by the fistful, which sometimes had some good results (Longest 1969; Chongolnee 1978). But problems existed, too. Each fall more than 500 new international students arrived on campus and came through the Office of International Student Adviser (ISAO). Students arrived at ISAO every day overloaded with verbal and written orientation information that had turned to mush: there was too much paper, and too many things to do in too short a time. Often it seemed this orientation overload actually hindered students' cultural adjustment at the beginning of their stays here. Conversely, many could not attend the useful programs because of schedule conflicts. And many of them felt alienated and isolated in those first confusing days on one of the largest campuses in the United States. It was no wonder so many of their faces appeared at ISAO again, mid-quarter or mid-year, with academic, visa, or personal adjustment problems that had mushroomed.

Orientation programs should be tools to help international students meet their needs, overcome their problems, and adjust more easily to American life (Lee 1981). In 1974 members of the ISAO staff and other campus personnel worked together to devise an experimental orientation program (Moran, Mestenhauser & Pedersen 1974). The 20-hour weekend program used role plays and simulation exercises, and included foreign and American students as well as community volunteers. Some of the international students had just arrived, but others had been in the United States for more than a year. Together they explored various "images" of foreign students, based on their own and others' viewpoints. Given brief case studies, they talked through alternative solutions and learned to create their own. A statistical survey did not show significantly different results between the orientation group and a control group, but participants' comments gave a fuller and more positive evaluation of the program: they said it was a useful, mutual learning experience and they demonstrated how it had opened communication between different individuals and groups. The experience in evaluating the results of this experimental orientation program revealed the enormous problems faced in cross-cultural research. Despite a very sophisticated methodology, the statistical study showed no differences between the oriented and non-oriented students. Other evidence clearly suggested that there were enormous gains on the part of those who attended the special weekend.

The workshop methodology, based on Harrison and Hopkins' (1967) experiential learning process, maintained its appeal. Members of ISAO staff continued developing and teaching a course in the Department of Speech Communication, the Intercultural Communication Workshop. This course attempted to provide a complete learning environment in which participants were involved on both the intellectual and experiential levels.

The Orientation Program Design

The "Survival Orientation Seminars" (SOS) emerged from these activities in 1981. The author, appointed program director and facilitator, commenced juggling concepts, ideas, resources, and other campus realities. The general objectives followed Lee's: to facilitate international students' adjustment to life in a new culture, meet their immediate needs upon arrival, and help them form a support group among themselves. The last seemed especially crucial for the long-term results of the orientation program. The program hoped to attract 35 to 50 students to the seminar.

A great deal of attention focused on the facilitator's role itself. As facilitator, the author would prepare the experiential situations—but that was just the beginning. The students were helped to become more independent of external sources in making decisions, develop "emotional insight" for dealing with feelings, and learn to make choices in stressful or ambiguous situations. The facilitator's primary goals would be to help the group in "learning how to learn" by creating and maintaining a climate of confidence in themselves and their capacity to discover and learn that was essential at this time of cross-cultural change. To do this, various experiential training techniques (case incidents, role plays, small groups, etc.) were utilized for the subjects of each session. It would be critical that the facilitator keep a very flexible attitude about the outcome of each session: every group would and should be different in facing problems and solutions. This diversity should be encouraged rather than held in check.

Total costs of the seminar were covered by a fee paid by the participants and by a small grant from the university's Orientation Fees Committee. Brochures and application forms were sent to prospective students overseas. Those accepted were asked to arrive at least one day before the SOS starting date.

A campsite located in a forested area of a nearby suburb was selected for the SOS location. This would provide necessary separation from the daily life of the campus but allow the staff to travel back and forth easily and keep resources accessible. Dormitories and meals were provided.

The program would last three days. Activities were planned and scheduled according to five criteria: (1) breaking the ice and establishing the learning methodology and participative style in the initial session; (2) maintaining the importance of cultural identity as a necessary step in starting an intercultural experience; (3) recognizing the urgency of providing important informational items (housing, registration, etc.) to be worked through to relieve the students' natural anxiety; (4) combining cultural and informational items; (5) using other students and staff as resources for some of the sessions.

The first day would begin with an introduction to the program and then to the participants in an exercise called "Friendly Facts," specially prepared to break the ice through rapid search to discover within the participants facts like "who graduated from Sorbonne University with Honors?" It would be followed by a communication exercise, Identifying Cultural Values, to facilitate the expression and awareness of cultural diversity. The students would share in dyads the things and people they were going to miss while in the United States, which would help integrate emotional issues into the overall perspective of their educational development. It led into the next exercise, Fears and Hopes, about their new experiences. This discussion of similar interests and expectations was intended to develop a less anxious and more realistic attitude in facing new life in this culture. At the end of the day the students would participate in an Informal Discussion with American Students about current issues of American life. Some 20 American students would come to talk with them in small-group format.

The second day's schedule consisted primarily of topical workshops, on Housing, Registration (including a simulation of the actual procedure), Transportation (by metro transit personnel), Academic Advising in two subgroups for graduates and undergraduates, and Shopping. An exercise in the morning, Communication Across Cultures, would help the students experience and analyze barriers in intercultural communication, especially difficulties stemming from misunderstandings, exaggerations, and avoidance. In the afternoon about 30 international students who had been in the United States for more than a year would arrive for an Informal Discussion with International Students. In two subgroups, discussion would cover academic programs, social behavior, religions, American students, campus issues, etc. An evening bonfire, when a talent show facilitated communication and friendship, is still remembered today.

The third day would begin with a multiple role play, "Dealing with the System." The students would play the roles of international students vis-à-vis colleagues playing the roles of international student advisers and faculty, followed by discussion and analysis. A panel on Issues Concerning International Students would feature ISAO staff talking about immigration matters, work permission, health insurance, financial aids, counseling, and legal matters. Case Incidents in Cross-Cultural Adjustment would consist of discussions in small groups of situations involving international students. Then the plenary would review each case and the facilitator would integrate this into an overall review of the process of cultural adjustment, marking the end of the program. Finally, an Evaluation questionnaire would be distributed to the students to be completed immediately, and they would be driven back to the university campus.

Evaluation

Forty-two students participated in SOS, 26 males and 16 females. Most of them (30) were graduate students, but five were undergraduates and seven were adult specials (in non-degree programs). They represented 25 countries: Germany, Japan, Taiwan, the Philippines, Spain, Thailand, Uruguay, the Bahamas, Botswana, Brazil, Canada, Chile, Colombia, Ethiopia, France, India, Ireland, Israel, Jamaica, Korea, Malaysia, Nigeria, Norway, Singapore, and Sweden.

The experience was gratifying, after all the work and planning. The staff felt it successful, remembering various sessions they had helped facilitate or the spontaneous talent show and informal discussions at the bonfire with 70 international students. But would tabulating the questionnaires bear out the impressions of success?

Five criteria were used in designing the evaluation questionnaire to provide a comprehensive view of each activity: (1) level of information; (2) usefulness; (3) intellectual stimulus, or interest; (4) level of participation; and (5) level of enjoyment. A sixth category was named "Overall Rating" to perceive a holistic reaction to each individual session. The questionnaire used a scale of one to five, with one being the negative opposite of five (for example, five = informative, one = uninformative).

The tabulated data fell into two types of numerical results. The first type described how the general group rated each activity in the different characteristics of the learning environment and styles of the sessions (shown in Table 1). The second type described the ratings of each activity made by students from regions of the world, and is summarized in Table 2. This arbitrary division of the world into regions served as an exploratory study of different reactions to each activity by different cultural or regional groups. Even if the numbers for this second type of data are not statistically significant, they can provide some valuable data for further investigation.

TABLE 1
GROUP AVERAGES BY ACTIVITY

	Friendly Facts	Identifying Cultural Values	Fears and Hopes	Discussion with American Students	Housing Workshop	Communication Across Cultures	Registration Workshop	Academic Advising Workshop	Discussion with Int'l. Students	Role Plays	ISAO Panel	Case Incidents	Evaluation	Overall Rating
Informative = 5 / Uninformative = 1	3.5	3.5	3.7	4.0	4.3	3.3	4.7	4.1	4.5	3.6	4.5	4.1	4.1	4.3
Useful = 5 / Not Useful = 1	3.9	3.7	3.6	4.0	4.4	3.8	4.1	4.2	4.2	3.8	4.6	4.0	4.0	4.4
Interesting = 5 / Boring = 1	3.9	3.9	3.7	4.0	3.8	3.9	3.4	4.0	3.9	4.1	4.5	4.0	3.9	4.3
Participative = 5 / Noninteractive = 1	4.0	3.8	4.0	4.1	3.1	3.8	3.9	3.4	4.0	4.0	3.9	3.8	3.5	4.2
Enjoyable = 5 / Unenjoyable = 1	4.2	3.8	4.0	3.8	3.6	4.1	3.6	3.8	4.3	4.2	4.2	4.0	3.7	4.2
Overall High = 5 / Rating Low = 1	3.9	3.8	3.8	3.9	3.9	3.8	3.9	4.0	4.3	3.9	4.4	3.8	3.9	4.3

TABLE 2
GROUP RATINGS BY CULTURE GROUPS

	Friendly Facts	Identifying Cultural Values	Fears and Hopes	Discussion with American Students	Housing Workshop	Communication Across Cultures	Registration Workshop	Academic Advising Workshop	Discussion with Int'l. Students	Role Plays	ISAO Panel	Case Incidents	Evaluation	Overall Rating
Africa	4.0	4.0	4.5	3.5	4.0	3.3	5.0	4.3	4.0	4.3	5.0	4.3	4.5	4.7
L. America	3.6	2.8	3.0	3.4	4.3	2.6	3.8	4.2	4.4	2.8	3.8	3.0	4.2	4.2
N. America	4.0	5.0	5.0	4.0	5.0	5.0	5.0	5.0	4.0	4.0	4.0	4.0	4.0	4.0
C. Asia	3.5	3.0	3.5	4.5	3.0	4.0	3.0	2.5	4.0	4.0	5.0	4.0	3.5	4.0
E. Asia	3.9	3.4	3.5	3.6	3.7	3.8	3.6	3.7	3.2	3.3	4.0	3.5	3.9	3.9
Caribbean	4.5	5.0	3.5	4.0	3.5	3.5	2.0	4.5	5.0	4.5	4.5	5.0	4.0	4.5
N. Europe	3.5	3.7	4.3	3.3	4.0	3.8	4.3	4.2	4.3	3.6	4.3	3.6	3.4	4.0
S. Europe	4.0	3.5	3.5	5.0	3.5	5.0	4.5	4.0	5.0	4.5	4.5	4.0	3.5	4.5
Highest	4.0	5.0	5.0	5.0	5.0	5.0	5.0	5.0	5.0	4.5	5.0	5.0	4.5	4.7
Lowest	3.5	2.8	3.0	3.3	3.0	2.6	2.0	2.5	3.2	2.8	3.8	3.0	3.4	3.9
Median	3.9	3.8	3.8	3.9	3.9	3.8	3.9	4.0	4.3	3.9	4.4	3.9	3.9	4.5

It is important to note again in looking at Tables 1 and 2 that these numbers, while presenting important data in two different perspectives, are not statistically significant and perhaps reflect only individual reactions that cannot be generalized. On the other hand, further studies can be done with these data to search for similar reactions in other, similar experiences.

In addition, it is important to consider personal and cultural differences in judging program activities. Some individuals and cultures in general find it easier than others do to separate sessions and persons for analysis and evaluation. Some regional groups and individuals may tend to "overvalue" while others tend to do the opposite. The students' English fluency may also be a significant factor, especially in the very participatory style of this orientation program. Such programs are sometimes the first test of their capacity to deal with the foreign language, and their reactions and feelings could influence their objective analysis of the different sessions.

All these things considered, the participants gave most of the SOS activities very high ratings associated with the style and methodology of each session. In general, objectives were met, according to the students' evaluation questionnaires. SOS was a success. But it is difficult to measure the effectiveness of the sessions or the overall objectives of the orientation seminar without two things: a control group of similar international students who have not attended the program, and a follow-up evaluation of both groups at some intervals of their stay in the United States. Staff overload and insufficient funds prevent doing either. Even if they were implemented, however, it would still be difficult to evaluate changes in attitudes or levels of self-awareness regarding cultural issues (or even in levels of information for meeting immediate needs).

Further research can explore many of the issues left unresolved here, correct the inadequacies of the study, and expand on it. Research should also investigate more closely the experiential methodology as applied in the program.

When implemented among particular cultural groups, experiential participative training models raise many questions. Some may argue, for example, that "role plays" don't match with cultural tradition among Japanese students, and that perhaps Latin Americans are more inclined to participate in them. The data from this study, although limited, somehow indicated the opposite trend. The question should more properly be addressed to the results of the methodology rather than to the methodology itself.

If one still feels that orientation programs should be "informative only," then perhaps the long-used cognitive-centered pedagogy in intercultural programs remains the appropriate approach. The SOS approach has tried instead to include the experiential aspect, which promotes behavioral, self-awareness, and socioemotional learning. In this central moment of cultural transition, the integration of theory and practice is the goal.

Students must adjust to a multitude of situations coming to this country. It would be ideal to adjust orientation programs to each student's needs according to his or her pedagogical background. But our educational responsibility is to the overall needs of the whole international student population. We design orientation programs with the hope that the students will learn from our best intentions, as part of an educational institution.

References

Chongolnee, Burunchai. 1978. Academic, situational, organismic, and attitudinal factors affecting the academic achievement of foreign graduate students at Iowa State University. Ph.D. dissertation, Iowa State University, Ames, Iowa.

Harrison, Roger and Richard Hopkins. 1967. The design of cross cultural training: An alternative to the university model. *Journal of Applied Behavioral Science* 3:341–60.

Lee, Motoko Y., et al. 1981. *Needs of foreign students from developing nations at U.S. colleges and universities.* Washington, D.C.: National Association for Foreign Student Affairs.

Longest, James W. 1969. *Evaluating orientation for foreign students.* Ithaca, N.Y.: College of Agriculture at Cornell, SUNY.

Moran, Robert T., Josef A. Mestenhauser, and Paul B. Pedersen. 1974. Dress rehearsal for a cross-cultural experience. *International Educational and Cultural Exchange.* U.S. Advisory Commission on International and Cultural Exchange. Washington, D.C.: CU/ACS, U.S. Department of State.

Paige, R. Michael and Judith N. Martin. 1983. Ethical issues and ethics in cross cultural training. In Dan Landis and Richard W. Brislin, eds., *Handbook of intercultural training volume I.* New York: Pergamon.

Orientation for Americans

9

Survey of University Orientation Programs for American Students Going Abroad

Karen Rosenquist Watts

How do U.S. colleges and universities prepare students for study abroad? This is one of several important questions being abstracted here from a larger study of the institutional context of study abroad (Rosenquist 1986). That study examined the relationship between preparation programs and the types of study abroad programs for which they prepare students, the settings of the study abroad programs, and their perceived support from top administration. It also studied how institutions handle the study abroad programs themselves, and the relationship between study abroad programs and the institutions' structural characteristics (affiliation, student enrollment, and geographic location). The survey first asked questions about colleges' and universities' structural characteristics, then about their study abroad programs, and finally about their preparation programs for study abroad. Although orientation programs are treated outside their institutional settings, a brief description of the extent to which universities and colleges prepare their students for study abroad might be helpful to provide a frame of reference for other chapters that aid the readers in visualizing such specific programs.

A three-part questionnaire was administered to all 571 members of the Section on U.S. Study Abroad of the National Association for Foreign Student Affairs. Some 214 responses could not be used for meaningful tabulations; of the 357 that remained, 197 (55%) responded. Their comments are the basis of this chapter. Drawing on the results from the survey, this summary attempts to answer questions related to the extent, nature, kind, and content of formal preparation programs offered by the reporting institutions.

To set the stage, Table 1 shows that the number of study abroad programs of the responding institutions range from one to 60, with some 20 percent reporting no such programs at all. Almost 60 percent of those

TABLE 1

Number of Preparation Programs

No. of Programs	Valid %	Count
0	31.5	62
1–5	39.6	78
6–10	11.6	23
11–15	2.5	5
16–25	6.0	12
28–50	3.0	6
Informal Preparation	5.6	11
	100.0	197

Mean = 49

who have primary responsibility for these programs also indicated that they participate in cooperative arrangements with other institutions and their study abroad programs. The data also showed that large and middle-size institutions offer significantly more study abroad programs than do smaller schools. Generally, the programs are for long-term study abroad, with 45 percent indicating that their students spent an academic year abroad, while 38 percent call for a shorter stay of 3–6 months abroad. In addition, most respondents perceive their top administrators to be supportive of study abroad, with some 55 percent being reportedly very supportive, 33 percent somewhat or slightly supportive, and others either neutral or unresponsive. (Unfortunately this study, like many of similar type, has not been able to provide statistical data about the overall extent to which U.S. students study abroad, and the percentage of those who never do so.)

Preparation Programs: Who, What, How Often

Over two-thirds (69%) of the respondents indicated that their institutions provided their students who intend to study abroad with some form of preparation during the previous academic term. Still, over 30 percent provided none. The highest number of preparation programs offered by any one institution is 50; however, the mean number was 4.9 (See Table 1). The 62 respondents (31%) who indicated that their institutions do not provide any form of preparation for students going abroad were eliminated from the remainder of the investigation. The data analysis in this section, therefore, describes the methods of preparing students for study abroad experiences employed among 135 U.S. colleges and universities.

A high proportion (89%) of individuals indicated that their offices are directly involved in preparation programs. Slightly fewer (85%) said they are personally involved in administering or contributing to the administration of preparation programs. Respondents' principal assignments at their institutions are mostly (59%) as staff members; 18 percent of the staff members are study abroad advisers and 16 percent are associate/assistant directors of international programs. The largest proportion of staff members (41%) are directors of international programs. One-third of the respondents have dual assignments at their institutions as members of both their faculty and staff. Faculty members most frequently chose history/political science (24%) and foreign languages (22%) as their primary areas of academic interest.

The majority of respondents (85%) indicated that departments other than their own participate in their preparation programs. Foreign language departments and other academic departments are the two categories of participating departments that respondents checked most frequently (60% and 53% respectively). Ninety-two percent of respondents also indicated that other individuals in addition to regular faculty and staff members contribute to preparation programs. Of these respondents, 91 percent included students who have returned from abroad, and 63 percent indicated that foreign students contribute to preparation programs.

The largest proportion of participants (43%) generally hold preparation programs two to three times per year, or every academic term. Less than one-third hold programs once a year, and 21 percent hold them four or more times per year.

Preparation Programs: Format, Content, Methods

The greatest variation in the programs pertained to their specialty (see Table 2). Most (74%) aim at specific study abroad experiences. Many (40%) also said they offer one preparation program for all students going abroad, regardless of destination. Almost as many (39%) combine preparation programs.

As for general format, over half the respondents said their programs are highly intensive one- to two-day sessions. But 19 percent are seminars or workshops spread over four to six weeks, and almost the same total

TABLE 2
TYPES OF PREPARATION PROGRAMS
OFFERED BY INSTITUTIONS

Program type	%	Count
One program prepares all students	40.1	55
Programs aimed at general region	16.3	22
Programs aimed at specific study abroad experience	74.1	100

TABLE 3
FORMAT OF PREPARATION OF PROGRAMS

Format	%	Count
Sessions spread over 1–2 days	57.8	78
Seminars/workshops spread over 1–2 weeks	8.1	11
Seminars/workshops spread over 4–6 weeks	18.5	25
7- to 9-week course	8.1	11
11- to 13-week course	5.9	8
14- to 16-week course	5.2	7
Other	11.9	16

number are offered as courses (see Table 3).

In terms of the total number of contact hours the preparation programs have with students, the two largest proportions of respondents placed their programs into the 1–4 hours (39%) and 5–12 hours (40%) categories. Twenty-six participants (19%) indicated that their preparation programs have more than 30 contact hours with students.

Academic credit is granted for 28.5 percent of the programs, but in 60 percent of the cases attendance is mandatory. The preparation programs utilize a variety of teaching techniques (see Table 4), with discussions or panels as the largest proportion. By far the most (85%) are conducted on the home campus; 19 percent are held at the study abroad site. Others are held on affiliated institutions' campuses or local off-campus sites (11.1% and 5.9% respectively).

Respondents appear to implement a variety of instructional techniques in their preparation programs. The largest proportion (67%) conduct their programs in an interactive learning mode of presentations and discussions. Only a surprisingly small percentage (22%) uses the experiential method of simulations and exercises. Eighty-seven percent (27) of those who use this technique only do so 25 percent and less of the time. Among the 91 individuals employing the discussion technique, on the other hand,

TABLE 4
TEACHING TECHNIQUES

Techniques	%	Count
Discussion/panel discussion	67.4	91
Lecture	57.0	77
Slide shows/films	54.1	73
Case studies/critical incidents	34.1	46
Reading assignments	32.6	44
Simulation exercises	22.2	30

29 (43%) employ it between 26 and 50 percent of the time, and 33 (37%) employ it 25 percent or less of the time in their preparation programs. About half the respondents use passive/classroom modes of teaching, such as slide shows or films (54%), as well as lectures (57%). The majority of participants employing these two techniques do so only 25 percent or less of the time; 66 (90%) individuals spend this much time using slide shows, and 48 (62%) spend this time lecturing in programs. Many respondents also spend 25 percent or less of the time in prepration programs using such teaching techniques as reading assignments and case studies.

In terms of content areas, the majority of participants (73%) indicated that "survival" information is given primary emphasis in their preparation programs. Within this group of 99 respondents, 40 (40%) emphasize this content area 26–50 percent of the time, and 39 (39%) emphasize it 25 percent or less of the time in their programs. A slightly larger majority (75%) of participants demonstrated giving primary emphasis to information regarding cultural differences in behavior, values, and norms in their programs. Among these respondents, 56 percent estimate giving emphasis to this area 26–50 percent of the time, and 36 percent emphasize it 25 percent or less of the time.

Eighty-one individuals (60%) said they give primary emphasis to experiences that develop skills for cross-cultural interaction. Most (60%) who give emphasis to these experiences do so 25 percent or less of the time, and 27 (33%) do so 26–50 percent of the time in preparation programs.

Respondents were asked to rate their familiarity with several concepts that are sometimes taught in cross-cultural preparation programs. Most participants (71–75%) provided such a rating for each concept. An impressive majority of these individuals indicated that they are very familiar with all but one of the concepts listed. The item most individuals did not indicate being very familiar with was attribution theory (43 respondents said they are not familiar with it). The concepts with which the largest proportions of participants are very familiar include culture shock (89%), reentry shock (77%), stereotypes (71%), culture-general (65%), and ethnocentrism (63%).

Finally, respondents estimated the approximate percent of time they spend teaching those concepts listed in the previous question with which they are familiar. Fewer people, about half the respondents, answered this question. Culture shock is the only concept that a majority (56%) of individuals indicated teaching in preparation programs. Twenty-six (34%) of these participants said they spend 16–30 percent of the time in their programs teaching this concept, and 47 (62%) said they spend 15 percent or less of the time on it. Large proportions of respondents indicated teaching various other concepts in preparation programs. Sixty-five participants (48%) teach assimilation/adaptation.

Implications for Practitioners

A useful distinction gathered from the review of literature about cross-cultural orientation programs suggests that there are three types of these programs (Kohls 1987; Bennett 1986). The most common is "orientation," which is generally characterized by providing information about the new environment. It usually is the shortest program available. Next comes "training," which attempts to concentrate on the skills needed in a specific culture. It is often culture-specific, and employs experiential methods more often than the previous type. Finally, there is "education," which includes cognitive, affective, and behavioral aspects of living in another culture. It requires the most contact hours, and more sophisticated combinations of instructional strategies.

If one is to adapt this analytical distinction, it appears from the data that most universities and colleges do the best job with an orientation program; progressively less common are training and education.

Although preparation programs are common, there is a great deal that institutions can and should be doing to increase the levels of sophistication, improve instructional strategies to include experiential learning techniques, and integrate them with regular curricular programs.

References

Bennett, Milton J. 1986. A developmental approach to training for intercultural sensitivity: New applications for cross cultural orientation. *International Journal of Intercultural Relations* 10(2).

Kohls, L. Robert 1987. Four traditional approaches to developing cross-cultural preparedness in adults: Education, training, orientation, and briefing. *International Journal of Intercultural Relations* 11(1):89–106.

Rosenquist, Karen. "Preparation for Cross-Cultural Communication: A Survey of Methods Employed by United States Colleges and Universities." Master's thesis, University of Kentucky, 1986.

10

Something for Everyone: A Search for Common Denominators

Jan Felsing

In April 1984 the Office of International Education and Services (OIES) offered its first orientation program for University of Iowa students going abroad to study, work, and travel. Its planning, implementation, and evaluation required many decisions—some "classic," some peculiar to that university. A description of the decision-making process can be interesting and instructive for practitioners—those principally responsible for advising students who study, travel, or work abroad—and for researchers, providing a look at the real-world context in which advisers work.

Establishing a Need for an Orientation Program

The staff working in study abroad at the University of Iowa in 1984 was inexperienced and overworked. The central administration had cut the sole professional study abroad position in 1982 when the university experienced a major reduction in state appropriations. An OIES professional assigned to study abroad part-time and a full-time secretary were then told to maintain "essential services." Yet there was promise of future support. A new president and vice president for academic affairs arrived, both of whom had publicly endorsed the importance of international education. And a faculty committee's report called for a significantly more vital study abroad program.

It was in this context of heightened visibility and potential reward that OIES's staff considered designing a predeparture orientation program for students about to study, work, or travel abroad. But was such a program an "essential service"? Given all the work that needed to be done, should this particular project be given priority?

OIES's staff turned for guidance to a booklet published by the National Association for Foreign Student Affairs (NAFSA). A statement in the Section for U.S. Students Abroad entry of *NAFSA Principles for International Educational Exchange* caught our eye: "The program should include an orientation, both predeparture and on-going, which assists participants in making appropriate personal, social and academic adjustments." Although the statement was aimed at those who administer study abroad programs, OIES's staff interpreted it to mean that universities who failed to offer predeparture orientation for their students going to study abroad were substandard.

The NAFSA statement so well documented the need for a predeparture program that OIES's staff discontinued its search for additional expert opinion. We ignored the literature on cross-cultural learning theory with which we were unfamiliar. Nor did we conduct a survey — even a random one — to assess the actual learning needs of our particular student population. As we began the process of planning our orientation program, it became apparent that we knew very little about the students — their prior experiences, personality traits, characteristics of their selected programs, or the countries to which they were headed.

Surveying the Needs and Characteristics of Student Beneficiaries

The search for common denominators began with efforts to learn a little bit about as many as possible of the students contemplating an international experience. A survey conducted in 1983 on behalf of the Study Abroad Committee told us that an average of six students yearly went to Mexico and Qubec for summer language and culture study, ten to Spain and Austria, and 30 to France. Another ten students were going to France during the summer as part of a new comparative law program. A smaller number of students each year practiced teaching in either Australia or the British Isles or participated in a College of Dentistry exchange with Denmark, a teaching assistant exchange with French universities, an exchange with a Japanese university, or a Paris-based program specializing in film criticism. Learning more about these students and attracting them to the orientation program would require cooperation with the faculty members who directed the programs.

We estimated that about 30 students would enroll in study abroad programs organized by other U.S. or foreign universities or exchange organizations. Most of them would make at least one visit to our office to consult study abroad materials and solicit advice about program selection. To learn more about these students required waiting until spring semester, when students confirmed their plans.

OIES had administrative responsibility for university-wide reciprocal exchange programs, for which about a dozen students depended on us for predeparture information about the bureaucratic aspects of their programs (academic credit, financial aid arrangements, health insurance, passports and visas, housing, payment of program fees, etc.). Though destined to reside in different countries (in 1984, the countries of choice were England, France, Costa Rica, Mexico, Finland, and Australia), all these students faced the challenge of enrolling directly in a foreign educational system where success demanded swift adaptation to the host culture. The basic elements of a predeparture program, we believed, should meet the needs of these twelve students.

We also knew that about 200 students purchased International Student Identity Cards from our office each year, most in late spring and early summer. Many of these students would be participating in those formal study abroad programs already mentioned. Others, however, would be traveling independently, primarily to Europe, or participating in the work-exchange program sponsored by the Council on International Educational Exchange. Could OIES's orientation program offer anything of value to these students?

Program Content and Format

The basic components of OIES's program slowly took shape in our collective imagination. Virtually all of our audience, we assumed, would be concerned with travel — from the United States to their program sites, within their host countries, and to closeby areas. Information about passports, visas, customs, health regulations, air fares, exchange rates, packing, and tips for traveling safely and cheaply should be of interest to all.

Whether they wished it or not, all would represent the United States in their contacts with foreign nationals. To us, this meant that students should be relatively well informed about geopolitical events, understand their own culture well, and be aware that certain kinds of behaviors, although appropriate in our own culture, might be inappropriate in another. We wanted to encourage students to consider modifying those behaviors in advance.

Finally, we assumed that many students genuinely wanted to better understand the culture(s) of which they would briefly become a part. We believed it would be helpful if they obtained as much information about that culture as possible before their departure.

Students would not share the need for the same bureaucratic information, so we resolved to address these considerations in another way.

A number of additional assumptions and practical realities guided our decision making for the program's format. After discussing several alternatives, we decided to hold the program on a Saturday in late April. Meeting so late in the semester meant that we would compete with the upcoming final exams, but it would give us precious time to gather names and addresses of as many students as possible. We rejected the alternative — stretching the program over several afternoons, evenings, or Saturdays — as too demanding on staff time.

The day-long format also provided the occasion to serve a catered luncheon at the new Iowa International Center, a large congenial room adjacent to the OIES offices. By catering a French luncheon and selecting foods many of the students might not know how to eat á la française, we hoped to establish a link between the morning part of the program, which focused on travel, and the afternoon sessions, which focused on cultural adjustment. Students traveling to the same country would sit at the same table and converse with each other and with at least one recently returned student invited as our guest. At the same time, at least one person at each table would model "correct" table manners and engage others in discussion about them. We invited the university president for lunch so that he could meet and address the students.

After the luncheon and travel component of the program, we would clear the tables and set up the area for the three-hour *Bafá Bafá* exercise (Shirts 1977). The orientation program would conclude with students forming groups according to similar target countries or geographical areas. Here they would discuss those aspects of their new host culture that they could expect to be significantly different from life as they experienced it in the United States.

Because we knew that most U.S. students were unused to sitting for long periods of time and expected interesting as well as informative presentations, we resolved to supplement the traditional lecture approach with panel presentations, skits, and small-group discussions. We also recognized that it was impossible for us to tell students everything they needed to know in a mere eight hours. We decided to give each participant a packet of written materials that expanded on and supplemented the oral presentations. Because we had not already collected such materials to any great extent, we asked Dorothy Foley of Iowa State University to share copies of handouts she used in her "Tips for Travelers" workshop series. We would individualize the packets of information with culture-specific materials after students registered and we were certain of their destinations.

Program Staff

Because the part-time study abroad adviser and her secretary could not collect and present information for all aspects of the programs themselves, they enlisted help from others, mostly from within the OIES itself. Two foreign student advisers, one experienced in cross-cultural training, volunteered to take responsibility for *Bafá Bafá*. Three OIES student employees who had traveled extensively and had some familiarity with study, work, and travel abroad were assigned responsibility for one component of the program. This included researching topics to be covered, presenting the information, and collecting written materials about their topic to be included in the information packets.

We invited foreign students to participate in the afternoon sessions. Their presence was critical to the discussions about differences between the United States and a particular foreign country, we believed. We also suspected that the participation of foreign exchange students in the *Bafá Bafá* exercise would help them better understand their own experiences while in the United States.

We invited U.S. students recently returned from study, work, or travel abroad to attend the morning session and to be our guests for lunch. We knew that our presentations would be quite general and would focus on potential problems and safeguards against them. The presence during lunch of students recently returned from successful international experiences guaranteed the sharing of humorous anecdotes and specific travel information targeted at a given country or geographical area.

Representatives from local travel agencies were invited to discuss travel from the United States to the program site. About one week before the program, we gave each travel agent information about the destinations and dates of travel (but not the names) of each of the program participants.

Finally, we invited the faculty directors of the university-sponsored study abroad programs to join us. Only the director of the summer language and literature program to France accepted our invitation.

Budget

We knew that publicity, handout copies, and the catered luncheon would cost money that the OIES did not have in its budget. We rejected the idea of seeking special allocation from the central administration to support these costs. Because the bulk of the expenses would result from the catered luncheon, it seemed appropriate to assess this charge to its consumers. The registration fee also permitted prospective participants to assign a monetary value to the program and motivated us to "give them their money's worth."

We decided to charge a two-tiered registration fee: five dollars for the 9:00–12:00 p.m. travel session and ten dollars for the full day. Both sessions included a packet of printed information. We estimated our expenses somewhere around $200, and resolved to cancel the program and refund the registration fee if fewer than 20 students registered for the program.

We set the registration deadline two weeks before the program itself and decided to delay making copies for the information packets until we knew more about the program participants.

By the registration deadline we had netted $275 from the five students who registered for the morning session and 25 students who recognized the best value for their dollar — the all-day session. Fees collected from program participants paid for all expenses except staff time, but did not generate a surplus.

Evaluation

Program participants at the morning and all-day sessions were given a one-page questionnaire to complete and return before leaving. The questionnaire solicited opinions about the quality and quantity of information provided as well as the mode of presentation. It asked students to list topics they wished we had covered and those they wished we had not, to state whether they liked the all-day format or preferred several shorter sessions, and to give general suggestions for improvement.

The student evaluations were overwhelmingly positive, with once exception: the majority of students (15 out of 24) thought the presentation by the travel agents could have been improved. A debriefing session of OIES staff also elicited positive responses, although each staff member had suggestions for improvements.

Conclusion

We had measured students' and staff members' satisfaction with the program and found it to be high. But did our program have worth? Did it bring about certain, empirically verifiable changes in our prospective sojourners' behavior, changes beneficial to the individual or to humankind in general?

We never expected to accomplish such a feat. Our objectives were much more limited: to relay some basic information about the logistics of traveling outside the United States; to make students aware of the difficulties of describing and interpreting things unfamiliar and to discourage them from evaluating until they can at least describe them accurately; and to help them identify other people and written materials they could consult on their own. We provided an occasion for otherwise isolated students to share their excitement and apprehensions with others about to embark on a similar adventure.

It is important to acknowledge that not all of our objectives were oriented toward meeting the needs of the program participants, however. OIES chose to respond to key central administrators' increased interest in study abroad programs and services. We designed a highly visible "demonstration project" that showcased our talents well. Had we worked individually or in small groups with the dozen students participating in exchange programs for which we had administrative responsibility, we would not have succeeded in realizing these broader objectives nearly so well.

The process of planning and implementing the "Tips for International Travelers" workshop also taught us things about study, work, and travel abroad that we might not otherwise have learned, or learned so quickly. Our labor-intensive strategy brought about a kind of cooperation among OIES staff that does not ordinarily occur.

Hard work and high visibility — or perhaps simply greater institutional commitment — resulted in increased allocations for personnel and operating expenses at a time when other university departments were being asked to trim their budgets. We are now able to render a wider range of services to more people and to provide more opportunities for our own professional development. In the end it is to be hoped that students at the University of Iowa will be the beneficiaries.

References

National Association for Foreign Student Affairs. 1981. *NAFSA principles for international educational exchange.* Washington, D.C.: NAFSA

Shirts, R. Garry. 1977. *Bafá Bafá: A cross culture simulation.* Del Mar, CA: Simile II.

11

The Orientation Retreat: Preparing 200 Students for Study in 20 Countries

Sue K. Clarke

As study abroad advisers and directors of international studies programs, we must constantly evaluate how effectively we are preparing students for study abroad. Because our world is constantly changing, our preparation to learn about it must also change. But what guidelines can we rely upon as we prepare students for what will no doubt be one of the richest, most rewarding, most demanding, most life-changing experiences they will ever encounter — an experience that may affect other people in the world as much as it does them?

Encouraging an Attitude

As I reflect upon that question, one idea stands out in my mind. The best service we can provide our students is to help them develop an attitude that will hold them in good stead as they encounter new and unpredictable experiences. We must provide guidance and encouragement; we must also assume responsibility for provoking students' interest. We cannot hope to tell students categorically "how it will be," but we can give them information where possible and applicable. We have to trust that they can learn for themselves away from the lectures and discussion groups of any orientation program. Most importantly, we must encourage an attitude in which students recognize the importance of understanding between cultures. It is one in which students are prepared to:

- take their experiences in other countries seriously (as much more than a trip to an amusement park or a "shopping spree");
- prepare themselves in a practical way to study, travel, and live in other countries;
- keep an open mind, appreciating the diversity of our world without judging other people and cultures;

- accept the responsibility to learn more about themselves as Americans, about the United States, and about the way in which this nation affects other countries;
- show concern for other countries and their problems, and for the welfare of the world;
- recognize the interconnectedness of global issues (such as poverty, depletion of resources, overpopulation); and
- consider both their expectations for and commitment to this particular learning experience.

Encouraging this kind of attitude should permeate all the specific training we do to prepare students to study abroad.

Background: The Nature of Study Abroad Programs at St. Olaf

Each year St. Olaf College sends some 200 students to a variety of Western and non-Western countries to study for a semester or a year on programs of widely differing content and structure. In any given year, students might be studying in Colombia, Costa Rica, Egypt, England, France, Germany, Greece, Hong Kong, India, Ireland, Israel, Italy, Japan, Liberia, Norway, Papua New Guinea, the People's Republic of China, Spain, Taiwan, and Thailand. The content and organization of the programs is almost as diverse as the number of countries visited: in duration, from one month to a full academic year; in educational approach, from admittance to a foreign university to taking courses taught by an accompanying St. Olaf faculty member; in numbers, from a single individual studying abroad to 25 or more students traveling and studying together; in accommodations, from native homes in Thailand to a dormitory in India or Taiwan, a hostel in Jerusalem, or a temple in Japan. In addition, some programs are introductory and others have extensive prerequisites. How does one structure orientation to meet the needs of such varied programs?

Schedule of the Retreat

To focus students' attention on the issues to be discussed, a series of questions is printed on the front of the orientation schedule sent one week prior to an orientation retreat:

- What does it mean to be an American?
- How are my values shaped by my culture?
- Where am I going, and what is that culture like?
- Why am I going?
- What do I hope to learn?
- What am I willing to risk?
- What do I have to offer?
- How do I prepare?

Students are also sent orientation handbooks specific to their study abroad program. Portions of the handbooks are written and revised by faculty and returned students. These are to be read in preparation for the retreat.

The retreat itself is divided into nine sessions to explore these questions. Large general sessions for the entire group are alternated with small group meetings for individual programs. Coffee breaks, meals, and a recreation session provide a change of pace in what proves to be an intensive weekend.

Session I: Keynote Address (15 minutes). The first session is a plenary meeting, including a welcome and keynote address by the director of international studies. The address sets the tone for the weekend by making the focus of the retreat explicit: to help create in students, faculty, and administrators alike a better understanding of their own culture and of other cultures. It begins with a definition of culture and continues by drawing a distinction between gaining "information" about the cultures and striving for "understanding" of other people in the world. Finally, it offers students the challenge to accept the major responsibility for shaping their study abroad experience themselves.

Session II: *Bafá Bafá* Simulation Game (Two hours). The simulation game *Bafá Bafá* (Shirts 1977) is the weekend kickoff. It creates two very different cultures, setting the stage to discuss building culture sensitivity and understanding culture shock. With 200 people at the retreat, at least five sections of the game run at once. The resource people leading the groups are carefully selected and trained to facilitate the game playing and to lead a follow-up discussion.

Session III: Slides/Practical Details (One hour 30 minutes). Past program participants make separate slide presentations to the small program groups. The slides and commentary focus on the people, places, and experiences that make the program a memorable and worthwhile personal and educational experience. This is also an opportunity to begin discussing practical details, such as dress, weather, health concerns, sites to visit, and people to meet.

Session IV: Images of the United States (One hour 45 minutes). If students are to have some understanding of other cultures, they must know something about their own cultural heritage. In this session, a faculty member with expertise in American studies lectures to the entire group. Items discussed include: What are American characteristics? Is there a typical American? Are you a typical American? How does the rest of the world see us, both as a nation and as individuals? Where do people in other countries get their information about us? How will who you are affect the way you interact with people in another culture? Following the presentation, returned students lead small discussion groups to expand upon issues and ideas raised.

Session V: Socio-Political Scenarios (One hour 10 minutes). During this set of meetings, distinction between the European and non-Western groups is very clearly made. The session consists of two large, simultaneous presentations. In "The Face of Europe," the presenter, a political science professor with expertise in comparative European politics, provides background information on such topics as NATO, the European Economic Community, East-West tensions and nuclear disarmament, and left-wing politics. The non-Western presentation, "Non-Western Cultures As Seen through Male/Female Roles," explores relationships between the sexes as well as other topics related to the specific countries in which the students will be living and traveling. It helps to sensitize students to cultural differences and, more specifically, to ways American men and women can conduct themselves to avoid offending people or putting themselves and their companions in uncomfortable or dangerous situations.

Session VI: More Practical Details (One hour). Students meet in small groups to address the practical dimensions of the experience. Faculty advisers and returned students act as resource people in reviewing items in the orientation handbook. Practical details, such as transportation, packing, protecting passports and other valuables, and program/college policies and procedures, are discussed.

Session VII: Area Specific Sessions—Current Events and Trends (50 minutes). It is embarrassing to suggest that enough information can be given in two one-hour sessions (Sessions VII and VIII) to appropriately introduce students to a country. However, given the time constraint, an attempt is made to provide some background information for students about the countries they will visit, intending that they build on this introduction with their own reading. Faculty members and students with expertise on specific countries leading these sessions focus on current events, realizing that the major concerns of a people are shaped by their history, geography, natural resources, government structures, and culture. Leaders are asked to consider (1) current happenings/issues of international concern; (2) the state of the economy and natural resources on which it is based; (3) the state of the current political structure; (4) human rights concerns; (5) distribution of the population; (6) health and welfare systems; (7) the stage of technology; (8) major concerns about and ties with the United States; and (9) military organization and how it is viewed by the public.

Session VIII: Area Specific Sessions—Building Cultural Awareness (One hour). The more aware students are of characteristics that shape the

85

cultures and people they meet, the more able they will be to successfully understand, communicate, and enjoy their experience. Topics suggested to leaders for consideration in organizing their remarks include (1) the social structure of the area (ethnic, professional, educational, family); (2) the roles of men and women; (3) religious philosophy and practice; (4) popular art, music, and architectural forms; (5) foods and eating etiquette; (6) values; (7) social practices; (8) education; (9) language; and (10) communication and media.

The European programs have a slightly different format. Since most of these students have taken courses in the language, literature, and culture of the country they will visit, the session enlarges on this previously acquired information. The students are encouraged to talk about manners and morals, the university system, and the country and its people in general.

Session IX: Expectations and Commitment — Small Group Discussions (One hour). It is important for students to explore their expectations for and commitment to the study abroad experience. Some students will have given considerable thought to these issues, while others will not have thought about them at all. Some students and faculty may resist participating in this kind of session, yet it is critical to consider these issues.

It is useful to begin the session with a discussion of the students' hopes and fears. One way to proceed is to ask students to make two lists. The leader, protecting their authors' anonymity, collects and surveys the lists, putting the hopes and fears in general categories. The leader talks about how to alleviate fears and realize hopes, which can lead naturally to a discussion of commitment. Such a discussion clarifies the need for following program policies and procedures, understanding cultural differences, and developing skills to adjust to another culture. Students also recognize that their hopes and fears are shared by others. This is often a first step in helping them gain self-confidence and a positive outlook about the study abroad experience that lies ahead.

An alternative approach is to ask a series of specific questions, such as: What academic goals do you have? What do you expect of the culture? What do you think the culture will expect of you? What do you expect of your group and of your group leader? What concerns do you have about going abroad?

For students who will be spending most of their time with a group, it is important to talk about the issues specific to the group experience: the physical closeness of the group, the need for privacy, the resolution of disagreements, the need for open communication, individual freedom, responsibility to the group, and support systems. Activities should be planned to help group members get to know each other well in advance.

Follow-up. During the weeks following the retreat, additional meetings can be held to continue discussions and present new topics if necessary. It is important for the groups traveling together to continue developing an *esprit de corps*. Program advisers are encouraged to provide reading lists and handouts. Those program groups accompanied by a St. Olaf faculty member will continue to have orientation meetings on site as they encounter new situations and new countries.

Selecting and Training Resource People

At St. Olaf College, every study abroad program has an assigned faculty adviser who is expected to participate in the retreat and is ultimately responsible for the students' orientation. Field supervisors (faculty members accompanying study abroad groups) are also key participants.

Carefully selected returned students also participate in the retreat. Departing students generally place great faith in the advice of their peers; however, the returned students must be cautioned against assuming that the new students' experiences will be exactly like their own experiences in the host country. Students on site often become concerned when their experiences do not match the stories they have heard. Returned students are therefore briefed about methods of presentation that are helpful and those that might be detrimental to the orientation process.

Resource people must be prepared to lead the sessions at the retreat. The committee may come up with an excellent schedule addressing the major orientation concerns, but the results will be less than positive if the faculty and students presenting and leading the discussions are not prepared. Despite their expertise, faculty and student leaders alike welcome and benefit from a set of written guidelines for each session. In addition, it is important to meet collectively before the retreat to clarify duties and discuss strategies for leading small group sessions.

Overall Effectiveness

The orientation retreat for St. Olaf students, in its seventh year at this writing, has received good reviews and is generally considered successful. One of the strongest aspects of the retreat format is the impact it makes on a student to see some 200 students planning to study abroad, along with 50 resource people, gathered together to help each other prepare for the programs. Students come away from the retreat feeling that theirs is an experience worth preparing for, one that promises to be exciting and enriching and one they can share with others on their return to the United States. Another advantage of the retreat format is that it takes students and faculty off campus for a concentrated period of time, away from their dorms and offices. They make a commitment to be present at all sessions.

Despite its general success, however, there are particular concerns that must be kept in mind. After running a retreat for several years in a row, there is a danger in becoming too comfortable with its format and content. New people must constantly be pulled into the retreat planning process to ask questions and contribute ideas. Here are some specific issues for careful consideration:

• Cultural differences are very apparent to the students going to non-Western cultures. However, the European groups, especially the England groups, sometimes belittle the importance of discussing cultural differences. They may argue that orientation is a waste of time for them because the European cultures will not be that different from their own American culture. But conversations with returned students confirm that they do need the orientation and are willing to admit it once they have returned. These students can make good suggestions as to topics to include in an orientation. It can be intriguing to explore cultural similarities, as well as subtle and not so subtle differences.

• When an orientation program is so large that many different groups are meeting at the same time, the director must depend on an extensive list of resource people to lead and direct discussions. Some leaders will be more inclined than others to devote time and attention to the details of an orientation and to their own preparation for it. All leaders and resource people, excited about their own experiences living and studying in other countries, will often talk rather than listen to the concerns of the students they are guiding.

• The fact that the number of study programs is large and the content diverse creates other special problems as well. How does one (a) plan to cover all of the country-specific information necessary in a limited amount of time, (b) provide resources for those programs that include only one or two students and help them feel part of the large group as well, (c) offer sessions that seem important for the entire group to hear while making sure that those sessions are applicable to each individual program, and (d) give students a chance to participate and ask questions?

• Finally, a balance must be reached between building skills that will help students live successfully in other cultures and providing facts and information about other cultures.

The Challenge to Students

In the end, our most important goal is challenging students to accept responsibility for shaping their own study abroad experience. Students must realize that they will get out of the experience what they themselves put into it. We as advisers must also impress upon students that their actions will make a difference in our world. They have a special opportunity to learn something as a result of their international experiences. What they learn or do not learn will have international implications because we are living in an interdependent world. And in that interdependent world the interpersonal communication between individuals may, in the long run, be more important than the relationships between nations or governments. The words of former Secretary of State Cyrus Vance set the challenge before us:

> The mystery for the historian of 1990 . . . will be why we reacted against change in the world and did not seek to shape it. The historian will then conclude that ours was a failure not of opportunity but of seeing opportunity; a failure not of resources but of the wisdom to use them; a failure not of intellect but of understanding and of will (Bonham 1980).

References

Bonham, George W. 1980. Education and the world view. *Change*, May–June, 3.

Shirts, R. Garry. 1977. *Bafá Bafá: A cross culture simulation.* Del Mar, CA: Simile II.

89

12

A Three-Tiered Approach to Cross-Cultural Orientation for U.S. Students Preparing to Study Abroad

Joseph O. Baker

A Brief History of Study Abroad
and Orientation at Brigham Young University

Brigham Young University (BYU) started sponsoring study abroad programs with a language group to Mexico in 1958. In the early 1970s it expanded to include year-round programs to London, Paris, Madrid, Vienna, and Jerusalem. It has added numerous two-month spring/summer programs and discontinued others. In 1983–84 over 700 students in 28 separate groups studied in Asia, Mexico, Canada, Great Britain, Europe, and the Middle East.

Study abroad programs sponsored at BYU are organized on campus, with academic departments and centers assuming academic accountability and recommending faculty directors. Each program is budgeted to sustain one faculty member per 15 students. Salaries and instructional costs are absorbed within the regular university budgets. A major objective of the programs is to provide opportunities for faculty as well as students, so BYU faculty always accompany groups and frequently provide some if not all of the instruction.

Nearly 80 percent of the students participating with BYU abroad are fully matriculated day-school students. Some drop out of school during the semester before departure to work, so only about 60 percent of any group is on campus during the semester before departure. This of course complicates any campus-based orientation program.

About 85 percent of most groups are women between the ages of 19 and 23. There are relatively few young men on most of the "non-specialized" programs.[1] One of the reasons for this is that, traditionally among Mormon families, most young men when they reach 19 volunteer for 18 to 24 months of service as missionaries, and may be sent to any one of over 180 missions throughout the world. Although young women are invited to serve, most do not, but their interest in "things international" is heightened because of the brothers and friends who are serving abroad.

The justification of a university to sponsor such study abroad programs lies in the belief that interaction with other peoples often improves intercultural understanding, enhances sensitivities and tolerance for others, and enriches the lives of students and faculty. The following goals reflect the vision and purpose of BYU's programs:

1. *To involve students with people of other cultures in spiritually rich learning situations that encourage personal relationships with new friends from abroad and thereby provide opportunity for personal and spiritual growth.* BYU students attend and participate as members in regular worship services and youth activities, and otherwise interact with a large number of "immediate friends" (usually members of the Mormon faith) in the foreign settings.

2. *To provide unique opportunities for personal growth and character development through extended residence in a foreign culture.* Students are encouraged to expand their capabilities by participating in situations unique to studying abroad and assuming duties and roles of getting along in a foreign environment. They are expected to keep journals wherein they evaluate themselves and analyze their growth.

3. *To provide learning opportunities that cannot be made available on campus but that are necessary to fulfill many departmental and college academic objectives.* Academic units on campus encourage specialized projects peculiar to their disciplines. Broader general education objectives are assisted by courses written especially to take advantage of the foreign setting.

4. *To provide meaningful professional development opportunities for qualified faculty.* By using BYU faculty with each program, more teachers are able to have a foreign experience whereby they enhance their scholarship and teaching in their regular campus assignments.

5. *To provide a program in which students desiring studying abroad can do so under high moral, ethical, and religious standards.* Serious and qualified students are able to find a "packaged" program that is academically appropriate, attractive, and economically feasible, and at the same time controlled by high standards of leadership and conduct.

6. *To provide on-campus classroom enrichment for the students who are unable to participate in study abroad.* Returning faculty and students enrich the classroom experience through their enthusiasm for meaningful learning and by exchanging and sharing ideas and experiences.

Orientations at BYU have been simple, complex, successful, and in some cases, nonexistent. On the earliest programs, students had the benefit of competent but anxious faculty who managed to communicate basic essentials sufficiently well to get the groups out and bring them back again.

The earliest programs were sponsored by language departments and had no formal structure for orientation outside of the language classroom. As the programs were repeated, some gradually became institutionalized, with interested faculty or even an entire department or college committee offering counsel on policies and guidelines. Administration and logistical detail was left to a fledgling study abroad office, but the actual task of preparing the individual student was still left to the often inexperienced faculty director, who was all too frequently untrained in cross-cultural learning.

Gradually, the study abroad office assumed by default more than design the role of orienting the students. In the beginning personnel were still untrained, but materials were collected, a handbook was written, and meetings were held. Experience was a good teacher, and the content of handbooks and handouts became more structured, specific, and relevant. Attempts were made to involve more qualified professionals to lecture and teach. But these efforts, too, were sometimes sporadic and seemed to lack relevance for the anxious student concerned more with packing and shopping lists.

Orientation Philosophy and Practice

Orientation should provide meaningful preparatory information and learning experiences for students going abroad. The "what" and "how" of this statement has changed substantially with experience. At BYU, attempts at meaningful orientation now tend to fall into three conceptual types or levels: (1) orientation for operational survival (logistics, finances); (2) orientation for course work (lectures, reading lists, assignments); (3) orientation for cross-cultural learning (skills, tools, and attitudes).

Orientation for Operational Survival. This level traditionally has taken the bulk of "orientation" time with students, when in reality it can often be more effectively handled in alternative ways. The tendency has been to try to get the students together and tell them what one thinks they should know about schedules, deadlines, costs, what is included in the "package" and what is not, and how to get passports, visas, and International Student Identity Cards.

Among the shortcomings of word-of-mouth communication in "orientation" meetings is the danger of miscommunication. Students tend to understand clearly only those items that they anxiously relate to immediately. Then there is the problem of getting the word out to off-campus students, or communicating clearly to those who, for one reason or another, did not attend the meetings where "everything was explained in detail."

Obviously an efficient system of written communication covering objectives, policies, rules, guidelines, and suggestions along with frequent updates, deadlines, schedules, changes, and hints is absolutely essential to any meaningful orientation program. At BYU information is distributed through a combination of brochures, handouts, and weekly meetings.

The brochures are the normal program flyers developed for promotion. They contain general information such as itinerary, academic emphasis (with list of available courses and brief content descriptions), prerequisites, cost estimate, and general promotional paragraphs.

The handouts usually take two forms: materials that the faculty feel appropriate to meet program objectives, and the rather formal "Notes from the Office" that contain basic information common to most groups, distributed weekly during the seven to ten weeks prior to departure.

The weekly meetings are held during the last "term" (half semester, seven weeks) before departure. During the first of two hours, all students in all programs meet together for a series of lectures and skills orientation designed to facilitate the transition into a "foreign" culture. These are broad and generic in nature and become part of the academic introduction explained below. The second hour is conducted by the faculty directors and is individualized with discussions, panels with returned participants, films, and slides.

In each group someone takes copious notes of all discussions, decisions, and recommendations that are not already contained in other handouts. These are processed and distributed the following week. If a student is unable to attend a weekly meeting, the packet for that week is mailed to him or her. Thus all students receive the same information, whether or not they are able to attend the sessions in person.

All applicants receive a looseleaf binder containing a handbook, sectional dividers, and instructions on how to organize and retain the subsequent information that they receive in the mailings. This collection becomes a valuable reference resource throughout the program.

Orientation for Course Work. The participants need a basic introduction to the host country, people, and culture to help them adapt and find meaning in their experiences, friendships, and discoveries abroad.

A series of lectures, films, and discussion groups, led either by the director or qualified guests, often works well. Absentees are still a problem. Reading lists are essential, but without tutoring they sometimes become laborious and discouraging. Structured courses for credit are good and solve some problems, but make no allowance for students signing up after registration or for off-campus enrollees.

BYU uses a combination of a formal independent study course specific to the host country, reinforcement through a weekly lecture series, and informal panels, presentations, and discussion groups. Students are

93

registered for one hour of credit in international relations and, in addition to the seven general lectures referred to above, are expected to complete the independent study course for the geographic area and culture where they will be living.

These courses are written by our own faculty, who have directed groups before, and stress the basic and essential information to begin a meaningful study experience abroad. Emphasis is light on detail and heavy on familiarization with the country, city, transportation, educational and social systems, customs, and expectations. These courses are administered through the BYU Department of Independent Study. Each director grades his or her own students and thus becomes better acquainted with their interests, abilities, personal objectives, and expectations.

Orientation for Cross-Cultural Learning. This is the area of orientation most frequently neglected in campus programs. Sooner or later we realize that in addition to all of the above, students need help with basic communicative skills, learning attitudes, and patterns of perceiving and interacting within different cultures. The need for training and developing cross-cultural learning skills goes far beyond the usual counsel for surviving "culture shock." Students need help coping with shifting views of themselves and learning how to adjust positively to a new understanding of just who the "outsiders" and the "insiders" are — who and what is "foreign," and why!

BYU is now testing a course that should be meaningful and appropriate for all students going abroad. It emphasizes how one learns and effectively interacts with other peoples in their cultural settings. It handles reentry ideas and skills that influence posture with neighbors and friends in our own culture.

The student is told that the sequence of orientation includes the intercultural skills section included in the handbook plus the area-specific course as an insert. All receive the same handbook, but the supplementary course varies with the program for which the student is applying. As these two parts are refined, we hope they will lose sharp distinguishing features and begin to anticipate the lessons of each other. That is, there will be more intercultural skills taught in the area-specific courses.

At present the course consists of six units: (1) Developing Empathy, (2) Suspended Judgment, (3) Essential Etiquette, (4) Culture Shock, (5) Nonverbal Communication, and (6) Language Barriers. Each unit is divided into a reading list,[2] a summary of basic concepts to be learned and understood (these are essentially objectives of the unit), some specific skills that each participant should strive to develop, and a list of tasks or assignments designed to help develop the skills and teach the concepts. These are generic in nature and designed to be appropriate for all students going abroad to whatever country or culture.[3]

A fairly rigorous, objective, and task-oriented program teaching intercultural skills, tools, and attitudes that would be appropriate and applicable in any culture should be required of all who would go abroad to study.

Conclusion

BYU's three-tiered approach to orientation features (a) logistical, financial, and tactical information, (b) academic readings and briefings in preparation for area-specific course work, and (c) the development of cross-cultural and intercultural skills that facilitate learning abroad and equip one to adjust to cultural differences throughout one's life. The world is changing, students are changing, and programs and orientations must keep changing and improving to help people get along and live fuller and richer lives together on this planet we all share.

Endnotes

1. Men have a higher ratio of participation in internships and single curriculum programs; thus the overall ratio in 1983–84 programs was 464 of 703, or 67 percent women.

2. At present we are using primarily BYU-produced *Culturgrams* and *Inter-Cultural Communicating*, with frequent references to other recommended resources, including Seymour Fersh, *Learning About Peoples and Cultures*, McDougal, Littell & Co., 1982, and L. Robert Kohls, *Survival Kit for Overseas Living*, Intercultural Network/Systran Publications, 1979.

3. This course is not marketable as yet and is being used for the first time in draft form for BYU students leaving for Europe in January 1985.

References

Fersh, Seymour. 1974. *Learning about peoples and cultures.* Evanston, IL: McDougal, Littell & Co.

Kohls, L. Robert. 1984. *Survival kit for overseas living,* second edition. Yarmouth, ME: Intercultural Press.

13

Orientation Development Project at the Experiment in International Living

Julie Soquet

This paper is intended to describe an orientation model developed by the Experiment in International Living (EIL) as a part of the Orientation Development Project funded through the President's International Youth Exchange Initiative of the United States Information Agency. The model addresses orientation as an ongoing process, with special focus on Part II: Group Orientation, which is designed for the pre-field experience. Considerations in the training of leaders to implement this phase are also addressed.

Background

The Orientation Development Project was funded to respond to needs of international youth exchange programs, for an improved training and orientation design, and for accompanying materials. Materials were developed for both participant and leader to assist with orientation implementation. The project stresses process as well as content, in the belief that participants can learn on their own if they have the means and support to do so. Leaders are trained to prepare participants to utilize their entire experience as a learning laboratory. Key aspects of the orientation plan include (1) integration of language acquisition and culture exploration within the same basic training concept; (2) emphasis on the process of learning throughout the entire experience, with group orientation as a time to prepare for the field situation; (3) experiential field approaches that utilize the homestay and in-country stay as a rich learning environment.

The project design and products reflect the input of the pilot groups, past EIL work in cross-cultural training, and contributions from the Peace Corps, American Field Service (AFS) International/Intercultural Programs, Youth for Understanding, other resources, and literature of the field.

Program Design

The program is divided into four phases that reflect the ongoing nature of orientation.

Part I: Predeparture Preparation. This phase is designed for home use upon acceptance to the program. Its goal is to raise questions in laying the foundation for the next phases: Who am I? Where do I come from? Where am I going? What do I know? (What will help me in this experience?)

Participants have opportunities to define themselves as products of their own language and cultural background, to see language as part of a communication system enriched with other forms of interaction, and to identify skills of which they may be unaware that will be useful in field situations.

Part II: Group Orientation. Ideally, group orientation is carried out by the leader and group who will be traveling together, just prior to the homestay or field experience. Part II investigates several questions: What have I brought with me? What information will help me? What will I need to be aware of? How will I adapt?

In this phase, participants are encouraged to become a cohesive group and to assume responsibilities as part of that group. The leader uses the group dynamic and the orientation plan as examples of how to learn from the immediate situation and transfer learning to upcoming cross-cultural experiences. The group looks at personal past learning situations and examines how they may apply past learning skills to their upcoming experiences.

Part III: In-Country Orientation. This part is organized as a guide and example of ways for participants to make the most of their field experiences. Activities may be organized by the group leader or by the participants on their own or with their host families. Sojourners are directed to learn the language by using all means available; to become sensitive to their own behavior within the family context and to be more aware of host family expectations; to find ways to enhance their knowledge and insights about the host culture; to try to resolve issues which arise; to become aware of the phases of cultural entry and adjustment; to be introduced to the notion of a multicultural world view; and to enjoy their experience to the fullest.

Ideally, the group comes together to provide support and encouragement to its members during this part. Sharing of experience and learning are often beneficial for everyone.

Part IV: Reentry. Reentry orientation begins before the return home and continues in the home country. It is designed to help participants recognize what has been learned from the experience; to identify cross-cultural skills that are relevant to other life experiences; and to encourage participants to think as global citizens.

Part IV, like Part II, is designed to be run by the group leader. The program evaluation may also be done at this time. Part IV is intended to provide a wrap-up to the experience and to begin the cycle once again, (re-)entering a culture in such a way as to gain the most from the experience.

A Closer Look at Part II: Group Orientation

A closer examination of Part II provides a more thorough understanding of this particular phase, and it also demonstrates the underlying assumptions, educational strategies, methods, and training ideas pervasive in the overall model. Part II is one of two parts for which the leader/group format is recommended.

Considerations for the Participant. With some modifications, this model and material can be useful to many groups and ages. The target audience is high school youth who, with a group leader, will be traveling to live with a family in another culture for a summer, semester, or year-long program. Formalized preparation is assumed to better equip the young sojourner to travel as a learner as well as a tourist. The kind of learning promoted through the orientation can be related to past learning experiences, and it can be enhanced to provide a useful approach for entering any new culture or miniculture. In this world of change, the adjustment process may also present effective ways to handle transitions and make the most of one's immediate environment. The ultimate goal is to create an intercultural and international awareness in ways that may contribute to world understanding and peace.

The orientation is geared toward entering a culture on its own terms, toward valuing cultural differences and trying to understand them within their context (culture-specific information, intercultural and language skill building, and adjustment issues).

Field Learning. Field learning requires that the individual assume more responsibility and self-direction than in a traditional classroom, where education is primarily teacher-directed. Accordingly, the participant should understand his or her motivation for participating in a program and compare expectations with the reality at hand. He or she needs to recognize the continual choice of being simply a tourist (observer) or a learner/tourist (participant). In addition, he or she must be willing to take risks, make mistakes, and to place himself or herself in the role of learner.

Field learning can be strengthened through the solid base of a cohesive group. Such a group does not just happen: it usually requires effort and commitment from all members and leader skills in facilitating the process. Carried to the extreme, the group identity can be counter-productive if it supersedes the individuals' interest and ability to interact fully with the new culture.

During the group orientation, the group dynamic can serve as a small laboratory of interactional and behavioral patterns. These may be used to point out examples relevant to intercultural communication in the field. To do this the leader must be so comfortable with the content of the orientation material content that he or she can pay attention to the group process.

The following field learning models were utilized to identify and develop the specific activities for Part II of the orientation model.

First, participants are caught in the midst of an unplanned event. Then they observe and reflect on what occurred. They develop a concept of what happened and why, test their concept in a subsequent experience, and thus set up the cycle again.

Learning through Experiential Approaches: Model I, based on David Kolb's (1979) experiential learning design, guides the educational processing of a spontaneous, unstructured experience.

Unplanned experience
e.g., buying a train
ticket to Genoa

Try out new idea
or new behavior
e.g., try purchasing
a ticket

Observe/reflect
e.g., observe others:
language, forming lines,
reading schedules

Conceptualize
e.g., consider how this is
similar/different
from your culture

Learning through Experiential Approaches: Model II, based on field problem-solving techniques (Kolb 1979), may serve well when participants would like to learn something specific from the environment.

Identify
what is to be learned;
e.g., how to shop in market

Evaluate
what has been learned
and whether the process
should begin again; e.g.,

1. feel you understand
   system
2. plan to try it on
   your own next day

Create
ways to go about
learning; e.g.,

1. go alone to market
   for host mother
2. go with host mother
   to market
3. go alone; observe
   others

Implement
way to get at information
e.g., ask host mother and
accompany to market

Select
ways to get information,
create experience; e.g.,
go with host mother

In the second model, participants identify the opportunity to learn in advance. They create ways to accomplish the learning and select an appropriate method. It is implemented and evaluated. If the original objective was accomplished, then that learning cycle may end. If not, then the objective may be redefined and the cycle repeated.

Resistance at any point on either model could present an opportunity, a choice to continue learning, to motivate oneself to take the necessary risk. Over time and with repetition, either model may become a spiral: participants can see the cumulative effect of what they knew before the program, what they learned during their experiences, and what can be carried into future experiences.

Content. The content sequencing is based on Maslow's (1954) hierarchy of needs and on the nature of orientations. Orientation programs tend to be filled with initial excitement followed by certain anxieties about survival information. The difficulty of the material increases as the program progresses.

We apply adult learning (andragogic) principles, remembering that adolescents are at a developmental learning stage that moves between abstract and concrete thinking in relating to their world. Activities are therefore designed to reflect both approaches to thinking and learning, as

100

well as different learning styles (visual, verbal, written, group, individual, active, passive).

The content traditionally covers subjects of other predeparture orientations for international youth exchange (AFS 1983; Youth for Understanding 1981) with the additional components of investigation of learning approaches, integration of language and culture, and particular concentration on field-learning techniques.

The orientation model is intended for a multicultural audience. Written by North Americans, it may reflect their bias, but it piloted through EIL's culturally diverse international network.

Evaluation. Responses to the materials have varied significantly depending on the program, the leader's attitude, and the underlying motivation for the student's participation in the program. Perhaps the least motivated are some of the summer participants, who feel the guided approach is too much like school and stifles their summer vacation. The motivated are those who receive enthusiastic guidance from their leaders.

The sessions in Part II are "Introduction to Orientation," "About Learning," "Fears and Expectations," "Program and Trip Information," "Host Country Information and Language," "Cross-Cultural Simulation," "Cultural Awareness and Skills," "Exploring the Community: The Interview," "Cultural Entry and Adjustment," and "Evaluation and Plan for Field Exploration." The sessions vary in length between one and three hours. Methods employed are presentations, exercises, and discussions.

Considerations for the Leader. EIL has prepared a separate guide for group leaders who accompany young people abroad. *Cross-Cultural Orientation: A Guide for Leaders and Educators* (Fantini 1985) suggests ways to handle the overall orientation, with special emphasis on Parts II and IV. To supplement the materials, EIL conducts one-and-a-half- to two-and-a-half-day training programs to prepare leaders to run orientation programs using the materials and models developed through the Orientation Development Project. This training has taken several forms over the years; it is now modeled after the content of Part II or Part IV. It provides leaders with the opportunity to experience the orientation so they are better able to decide how they will implement it to suit their style and the group's needs.

Leader training also emphasizes the process of facilitating discussion and building groups. The method by which leaders cover the material is crucial to its effectiveness. Leaders are encouraged to assume responsibility for sessions in the actual leader training. Learning can be heightened by less than perfect presentations. The workshop staff assign specific sessions to leaders and intervene to assist in debriefing the sessions for content and process.

Cross-Cultural Orientation: A Guide for Leaders and Educators is designed to help leaders implementing the overall orientation. Its second section, "Orientation Process," reinforces the underlying principles guiding the concept of the orientation and helps the leader with the process of guiding the participants through the experience. Specifically, "Orientation Process" provides information on differences between experiential and traditional learning, a comparison of andragogy and pedagogy, and considerations of situational leadership. Activities are included to enhance the understanding of these areas. Many leaders come from traditional teaching backgrounds and must translate their classroom skills to allow students to learn on their own instead of providing them with the answers. Only then will the leaders become successful guides of the field learning experience.

The Orientation Model: Problems and Considerations

While this model is designed to enhance the intercultural experience, some may argue that such a prescribed format may, in fact, inhibit the pure spontaneity of discovery. It is offered as a model, not by any means as a final word on how best to venture into a new culture. Additional evaluation of the final products' effectiveness is yet to be done. Time will tell whether the design has a long-term serviceability for the intended population. Thus far, it has worked well for the purposes of EIL's youth exchange programs, particularly with leader-led groups. The leaders' attitudes about orientation have greatly influenced the success of the program.

Conclusion

EIL has made steps toward integrating the language and culture components of the orientation process. Furthermore, experiential field learning in a group setting provides an opportunity to build group skills and learn from the resources provided by the group. Since most people often find themselves in some form of group (family, church, community, friends, committees, school projects), the orientation is pertinent to life after the program. It helps relate learning in a foreign exchange program to lifelong learning in all situations. EIL offers it as a model, one that may be refined for specific purposes and applied to other field learning situations.

References

AFS International/Intercultural Programs. 1983. *AFS orientation handbook.* New York: American Field Service. Intercultural/International Programs, Inc.

Fantini, Alvino, ed. 1985. *Cross-cultural orientation: A guide for leaders and educators.* Brattleboro, VT: Experiment Press.

Kolb, David. 1979. *Organizational psychology: An experiential approach.* Englewood Cliffs, NJ: Prentice-Hall, Inc.

Maslow, Abraham H. 1954. *Motivation and personality*. New York: Harper & Row.

Youth for Understanding. 1981. *Planning and conducting post-arrival orientation*. Washington, D.C.: Youth for Understanding.

14
Cross-Cultural Training in the Peace Corps

Roger Nicholson

Rationale and Overview

This paper discusses the Peace Corps's cross-cultural training in the eighties. The Peace Corps is committed to supporting experimentation and innovation in providing skills to volunteers that will enable them to adapt to different cultures and work successfully in development projects. A series of steps encompasses the overall approach to preparation of volunteers:

1. Systematic recruitment and screening processes incorporating a number of staging models used to develop readiness of volunteers;
2. In-country assignments to provide volunteers the opportunity to achieve the three goals of the Peace Corps:
   a. To provide technical expertise to requesting countries;
   b. To promote a better understanding of the United States on the part of the peoples served; and
   c. To promote a better understanding of the peoples served by the U.S. volunteers and the U.S. public.
3. Pre-service training, a skill development program scheduled prior to volunteer service that focuses on language and technical and cross-cultural training;
4. In-service training conducted during the volunteer service; and
5. Continuing support, advice, and technical assistance to volunteers provided by country staff.

The length of pre-service training, determined by the country staff, lasts from eight to twelve weeks. In 1984, the Peace Corps trained over 5,000 volunteers for 50 countries, and spent $20,000,000 in support of its various forms of training. Since its inception, the Peace Corps has trained 100,000 people.

History

The current system of cross-cultural training has evolved from twenty-three years of experience, and has changed from a lecture-format, area-studies methodology conducted in the United States in the early sixties to experiential, integrated training in the eighties.

From the beginning to the mid-sixties, training was conducted primarily in centers located in Puerto Rico, California, the Virgin Islands, and Hawaii. From the mid-sixties to the early seventies, training was conducted largely in the United States through contracts with universities and nonprofit organizations. Through the seventies and into the eighties, the majority of training has been conducted overseas, with the experiential approach prevailing.

The goal of cross-cultural training is to develop in volunteers an awareness of and sensitivity to foreign cultures that will enable them to successfully interact with host country counterparts and individuals in host communities. Consistent with the agency's mission, volunteers are assigned to jobs that require them to participate as functioning members of the community and contribute their skills to assist individuals on the road to self-reliance.

During the early years, training consisted of extensive area studies and simulation exercises designed to approximate living in a Third World culture. Contractors, largely universities, prepared cram courses on the politics, history, anthropology, sociology, linguistics, and economics of the host country and included some U.S. history and an analysis of American value systems.

In the early seventies, training strategies were determined to be irrelevant to the volunteers' actual living conditions and resulted in a low cost/benefit relation. An influx of returning volunteers employed as staff members and training assistants sparked an effort to better understand the volunteers' lives overseas and specific training needs. Major changes occurred during this period; particular emphasis was placed on training volunteers to learn how to work, actively participate in, and adapt to a new society and culture. Professional trainers directed and staffed these new training programs. Live-ins with host families were introduced, and cross-cultural training was based on the reality of living in the country of assignment. Thus, the training programs had three essential elements:

1. *A systematic organized approach* that related to the host country's developmental needs.
2. *An experiential, learning-by-doing method* that emphasized practical application skills.
3. *Talented trainers* familiar with the country, the assignments, and trainees' needs.

During the last few years, the Peace Corps has developed the following training resource manuals to provide generic training materials to assist trainers in all countries: "The Role of the Volunteer in Development"; "Working with Counterparts"; "Cross-Cultural Training Guide"; "Trainer Resource Guide"; "In-Service Training Manual"; "Close-of-Service Training Manual"; "Personal Safety"; "Health Guide"; "Older Volunteer Training Resource Guide"; and "In-Country Monitoring and Review System."

Assumptions

In order for volunteers to reach a level of satisfaction and effectiveness in the host culture, cross-cultural training provides entry skills as well as a framework for volunteers to measure their progress. The training is based on the following assumptions:

1. Certain cross-cultural skills and principles that have been identified and learned can be applied to the initial entry into an alien culture and to the process of becoming effective in that culture.

2. Effective cross-cultural training identifies prior experiences and skills, builds on them, adapts them, and introduces new skills. Thus volunteers are made aware of their reservoir of skills, habits, traditions, and knowledge that can be utilized in crossing cultures.

3. An emphasis on skill building creates independence and self-sufficiency and provides learning tools for continued active learning. Cross-cultural facts presented by experts (e.g., university faculty, former volunteers, designated host-country nationals) are generally ineffective in the long term, although comforting to the trainees in the short term. This approach has tended to create dependency with little personal meaning and is inclined to develop and perpetuate stereotypes. Cultural information is not discarded but becomes only one of the tools a trainer can utilize.

4. Cross-cultural training assumes a sequence wherein skills and principles are identified and built first, then practiced and refined in a training or laboratory environment, and finally applied outside the environment. In practical terms, this means that the program must be interspersed with sessions to permit trainees to reflect and assess their application efforts, receive assistance in refining their skills, and plan opportunities for further application. Only training sessions that focus on follow-up to the skill building are considered adequate.

The ultimate purpose of the Peace Corps's cross-cultural training is to assist individuals to participate fully, effectively, and satisfactorily in another culture. The preparation is not directed to outsiders who spend most of the time "looking at" the culture rather than living in it. Multiple benefits do, however, accrue to individuals able to observe their surroundings and take a step back to gain the knowledge and perspectives essential to living effectively in a different culture.

The cross-cultural component is of prime importance to the entire training program, since this element of the volunteer's experience is all pervasive. Thus, appropriate scheduling and priority are essential to cover this area in depth and detail.

Cross-cultural training must be viewed as one of three essential components of pre-service training, along with language and technical skill training. It is both an ongoing process, which begins during staging and continues throughout the volunteer's service, and an integrated process, with no single component conducted in isolation.

The Peace Corps bases its entire training-program design on the detailed analysis of volunteers' daily activities in terms of language, cross-cultural, and technical needs. This analysis includes every conceivable task a volunteer may perform. Cross-cultural training is incorporated into several stages preceding and during Peace Corps service.

Description of the Peace Corps's Experiential Training Process

The Peace Corps's innovative experiential training methodology incorporates a flexible program of activities, simulation exercises, and actual experiences. Trainees acquire knowledge and skills related to their work in a stimulating, relevant, and effective learning environment. This learner-centered, experiential approach toward training fits well the needs of the trainees to manage and assume responsibility for their functioning in often-remote assignments.

Experiential learning occurs when a person experiences an activity, reviews this activity critically, abstracts some useful insight from the analysis, and applies the results in a practical situation. The experiential learning process helps individuals to minimize subjective reactions and to draw out objective elements from their experiences.

Experiencing. A wide range of activities and exercises provides trainees with experiences from which they may extract the data to process and make generalizations. These include role plays, case studies, films and slide shows, and critical incidents.

Processing. During this crucial phase, individuals share with others their cognitive and affective reactions to the activities in which they have engaged and think through their experience to conceptualize reasons for drawing conclusions.

Processing helps the volunteers assess whether or not the previous training facilitated their learning. Techniques used during this step include group discussion of patterns and recurring topics and themes, generating and analyzing data, reporting, interpersonal feedback, interviewing, and participant observation.

Generalizing. This phase involves drawing inferences from the patterns and themes that have been identified earlier. Now the participants have the opportunity to identify similarities between their experiences within the training session and experiences that they anticipate encountering in the "real world."

Activities used to facilitate this generalizing step include summarizing learning into concise statements or generalizations, group discussions, identification of concepts, and individual and group responses to hypothetical questions related to the Peace Corps's cycle.

Applying. This step facilitates the learners' behavior modification. Drawing upon insights and conclusions they have reached during the learning process, trainees incorporate their learning into their lives by developing plans for more effective behavior. Techniques and activities used to facilitate the "applying" step include responding individually and as a group to hypothetical questions related to the geographic and cultural setting of the assignment and modifying and/or developing plans of action, personal goals, and strategies for personal behavior modification.

Summary

The ultimate purpose of the Peace Corps's cross-cultural training is to assist individuals to participate fully, effectively, and satisfactorily in another culture.

The training program initially emphasized university-based area-studies approaches to cultural orientation. During the seventies, the Peace Corps shifted to overseas in-country training that included short and long-term stays with host families as primary means of cultural interaction and learning. Today the Peace Corps utilizes a core curriculum of experiential learning activities that are integrated with language and technical training studies.

The Peace Corps's cross-cultural training utilizes an experiential, learning-by-doing method that emphasizes a practical application of learned skills. This process includes experiencing, processing, generalizing, and applying the lessons learned through the initial experience in "real world" situations. This process also requires sensitive trainers as facilitators to insure an effective and appropriate learning environment.

The Peace Corps has developed several predeparture assessment models for potential trainees, as well as stateside skill training, pre-service training, in-service training, and close-of-service training programs for trainees and volunteers.

15

The Navy
Overseas Duty Support Program:
An Organizational Approach to
Cross-Cultural Orientation

Sandra Mumford Fowler

An overseas transfer produces large-scale transformations and changes in the everyday life of individuals. These changes often involve new behavioral and internal responses, including new conceptions regarding the place of the self in the physical and social world. It is perhaps this demand for adaptation that creates the very vulnerable bond between the people and their organizations. This vulnerability underlies the demand that organizations take seriously the range of personal needs throughout the entire cycle of an overseas assignment.

To personal needs must be added the needs of the family. David and Elkind (1966) recognized early that mental health aspects of overseas effectiveness intertwined with the success or failure to establish satisfying family relationships in an unfamiliar social and linguistic environment. E.M. Bower (1967) studied American military and civilian families living in Europe and found that the phenomenon of "culture shock" was a real, significant fact of life for many families living in Europe.

The U.S. Navy instituted an intercultural relations program early in the 1970s that emphasized cross-cultural understanding, psychological adjustment, and diplomacy. In recent years the central focus of this program has shifted from fostering diplomatic relations to supporting the management of·the overseas experience as part of the individual, the family, and the organization.

Most large organizations both private and public attend well to the mechanical needs or relocation logistics of an overseas move. What has

NOTE: The opinions or assertions contained herein are the private views of the author and are not to be construed as official or as reflecting the views of the Department of the Navy or the Department of Defense.

gone unrecognized until relatively recently is that similar attention needs to be given to transporting emotions, attitudes, and coping skills. For an organization such as a branch of the military, this is a monumental task. Consider that there are over two million people in uniform, of which 24 percent are living overseas in at least 120 countries (Sinaiko 1981). When one adds accompanying family members and U.S. civilian support personnel, more than half a million Americans live and work abroad under the aegis of military service.

Since 1972 the all-volunteer force has continued to attract a wide spectrum of applicants through its promises of education, decent pay, travel, and security. These are the people the military assigns overseas to help carry out its primary mission to protect the peace. Service members enter into a "social contract" (Mumford 1983) with their military organizations when they receive overseas orders. In return for productivity and job performance, individuals expect a certain kind of life, lifestyle, and protection of person and property. The Navy has realized that a program of support is required to achieve these qualities in a foreign environment.

This paper will describe the Overseas Duty Support Program of the Navy as it is today and review its development, history, and organization. The literature derived from the program and cited throughout the chapter is in the public domain, available through the National Technical Information Service or directly from the Overseas Duty Support Program (NMPC-662), Washington, D.C., 20370-5662. This description is based on the author's responsibility for the Navy's program since January 1979.

Background

The roots of the Navy's program can be traced to the late nineteenth century, when ship captains directed junior officers to collect information regarding the foreign ports to be visited. More recently, President Eisenhower supported a "People to People" program that encouraged American servicemen to engage in individual acts of kindness. Chaplains frequently were called upon to organize good-will projects, such as painting orphanages, repairing hospitals, and delivering "Project Handclasp" materials. However, these isolated acts of kindness were not institutionalized, had no continuity, and in some cases were seen by host nationals as a means of soothing the American conscience.

The Vietnamese conflict provided a different context for intercultural relations. During previous wars there were compelling moral and humanitarian reasons for treating the local population with dignity and respect. In Vietnam, such behavior took on immense tactical importance as well. Coordination, cooperation, and trust were essential to survival.

In the early years of our involvement, there was little interest in training men in intercultural relations or the native language. In 1965, a Navy chaplain wrote a training manual explaining the Vietnamese religions and customs to lessen the growing friction between the Americans and the Vietnamese. This was the beginning of an ambitious attempt to change the attitudes of Americans serving in Vietnam. Sparked by two chaplains, the attitudes of 55,000 Marines were sampled and used as the basis for a three-day learning experience that included role reversal (a Marine would play the part of a Buddhist monk or Vietnamese farmer), simulations, and non-verbal drills. The training was designed to increase self awareness, tolerance of ambiguity, empathy, and self-confidence.

The Marines soon discovered that this strictly "humanitarian" project had a dramatic effect on operational aspects of the war. When two Marine regiments were compared, the regiment trained in intercultural relations recorded significantly more weapons turned in, booby traps and mines reported, enemy positions identified, and advance attack warnings from the Vietnamese villagers.

The chaplains also trained American members in combined action platoons (these included one squad of Marines and three squads of Viet-namese militia). The effect of the training was so obvious that the Viet-namese believed the trained Marines must have come from a different part of the United States. Also, as the pace of "Vietnamization" increased, it was found that the trained men were able to teach their counterparts to take over military tasks in far less time than men who had not received comparable training.

Following the Vietnam era, the organizational placement of the cross-cultural project experienced several major changes. Admiral Zumwalt established a Human Goals Program designed to improve the quality of worklife in the Navy. This program became the home of the Intercultural Relations (ICR) program. The chaplains who were so instrumental in start-ing the program were no longer integrally involved. Until 1975 as many as 66 ICR specialists functioned in 14 Human Resource Management (HRM) Centers worldwide.

In 1975, following a congressional mandate and internal Navy mainstreaming, the ICR specialists were integrated into the general HRM program, which also focused on equal opportunity, prevention of alcohol and drug abuse, and organizational effectiveness.

Initially the substance of the ICR program was clearly diplomacy, knowledge, and understanding. Some of the program activities consisted of:

1. Creating a predeparture training course for high impact personnel who would be in total immersion situations (such as the Personnel

Exchange Program). The goal was to make these personnel good representatives of the United States.

2. Developing a program to provide information and training for shipboard personnel who would have collateral responsibility for onboard programs designed to help officers and crew members have more successful and satisfying foreign liberty while reflecting well on the United States.

3. Designing a total overseas base program that helped orient members and families to live and work overseas and relate to the local community.

4. Researching selection and screening strategies to determine the best method for the Navy to ensure that only suitable, qualified personnel would be serving overseas (Yellen & Mumford 1975). *Bafá Bafá*, the cross-cultural simulation game (Shirts 1977), derives from this effort.

5. Determining unobtrusive measures to evaluate the success of overseas bases in integrating into the host country (for example, Fritsch, Meinken & Millerick 1973).

6. Surveying all the large overseas bases to assess levels of adjustment and satisfaction.

The early ICR program concentrated its training at the overseas bases. In some ways, this resembled the Peace Corps's in-country training paradigm. Keflavik, Iceland, and Roosevelt Roads, Puerto Rico, were selected as prototypes. The initial successes were highly reinforcing. At Roosevelt Roads a special course was developed for all military personnel; wives and school-age children were also encouraged to attend five eight-hour sessions devoted to changing the mainland Americans' attitudes toward Puerto Ricans. The Americans came to the course with all of their derogatory stereotypes firmly in mind. The results of the training were startling. Not only did the work of host employees on the base improve markedly (sick leaves decreased and efficiency increased), but so did the relationship between husbands and wives, and parents and children. The school psychologist reported fewer adjustment problems, and the mayors of the three closest towns reported fewer incidents between sailors and their citizens.

Despite early successes, the program was not without its difficulties. In July 1974, the Human Resource Development Project Office, which controlled the work of the specialists out of Washington, was abolished. The Bureau of Naval Personnel retained program sponsor/manager responsibilities, but all the specialists became part of the field chain of command. The Washington office lost its sizable staff and budget and its direct link to the field. At this point the entire ICR program had been developed as a response to specific conditions and needs almost despite the Navy itself. It had no specific mandate, legislated support base, or goals coordinated with other training objectives in related areas of race relations, drug and alcohol abuse, or leadership and management development. It became difficult to improve the program to meet whatever criticism was being voiced about it because there was no yardstick by which to evaluate and judge its effectiveness. Consequently it was difficult to justify its funding and staffing. It is always a struggle to obtain funds and people for a program that is not well institutionalized. Academicians will recognize the Navy's equivalent of the "absence of decisions."

As could be expected, the funding issue was resolved before policy. In March 1975, Admiral Bagley, chief of naval personnel, requested all commanders in chief and other upper echelon commanders to furnish information from the fleet to determine if the program was moving in the right direction and deserved further funding. As a whole, the responses were much more positive and supportive than had been expected. No one recommended a lesser effort, and almost everyone recommended expansion. The supportive nature of the responses had a decided impact, and the future of ICR in the Navy was assured.

With funding assured, the subsequent development of the program was characterized by goal setting, instructional strategies, and attempts to assess impact. The program changed its name to Overseas Diplomacy and had basically a three-pronged approach: the high impact personnel predeparture classroom training, the post-arrival programs at overseas bases, and the overseas diplomacy coordinator program for deploying units. These program developments were inspired and monitored by an overseas diplomacy coordinating committee, comprised of representatives throughout the Navy, that met for the first time in 1975.

The next major change in the program occurred in 1978 when the chief of naval operations changed the official name of the program to the "Overseas Duty Support Program" (ODSP), which remains its present title. By 1980, the management of the program had moved from an active duty commander to a civilian director. Based on a new instruction, the central focus of the program shifted from diplomacy to productivity and performance, from intercultural relations to cross-cultural skill-building and information that supports the individual management of the overseas experience.

The Current Program: The Overseas Duty Support Program

Assumptions. The structure and implementation of the current program rests on the following basic assumptions.

1. *The family is critically important.* Although the program was designed originally for active duty members, families now receive specific attention. Nice and Beck (1979) pointed out that the family and military are

113

in direct competition for the individual's loyalty and commitment. Even when a balance has been achieved, stresses on the family can put the two systems in conflict. One considerable stress is overseas assignment. Fisher, Wilkins, and Eulberg (1982) found that the success of a transfer is directly affected by the extent to which significant others provide social support during readjustment. Similarly, Torbiörn (1982) concluded that the most important factor in successful personnel adjustment is a positive attitude to life overseas on the part of the employee's spouse and family. Ever since a 1978 family awareness conference in Norfolk devoted a portion of its program to family needs overseas, the Navy has expanded its attention to the family. This changing focus resulted in March 1984 in the organizational realignment of ODSP under the Navy family support program.

2. *Positive, realistic expectations are the best precursors of a satisfying overseas experience.* Satisfaction can be seen as a function of the difference between reality and expectations. Information and training should be available to narrow a possible gap between them (Triandis 1981). A rapidly growing application of this concept, used by the Marine Corps among others, has been "realistic job previews" (RJPs). Review of RJP research reveals that RJPs are effective, and the results argue strongly for application of RJP techniques in preparation for overseas duty (Hayles 1981). A corollary that follows this proposition is that positive, preliminary appraisals of events during an overseas tour or foreign liberty are likely to produce positive outcomes. As an example, consider getting lost in a foreign city: with a positive, preliminary appraisal, one keys on the adventure of the situation and stories one will tell; with a negative preliminary appraisal, one may start blaming the culture for even simple discomforts, or feel helpless, hopeless, and angry (N.G. Dinges, personal communication, June 1981).

3. *Preparation and practice can make a difference.* This has both predeparture and post-arrival implications. Research in social psychology suggests that preparation for unpleasant events that could occur in the future reduces the severity of the impact. Aversive events are not a surprise; they feel like something one has planned for (Brislin 1974). Anxiety forces us into returning to old familiar ways and discarding new skills, techniques, and behaviors while under stress. A benefit of practice is that it makes new skills comfortable and reliable. The value of learning optional ways of behaving is that a person can choose the best method available, rather than the first that appears to fit.

4. *Classroom workshops, readings, or handouts are only the beginning of the process of learning to understand another culture.* Information exchange and classroom training are vitally important in themselves. However, Kraemer (1981) argues that such experiences alone may create the illusion of developing the participant's understanding of culture (which

might soon be shattered). Instead, he advocates that instruction should focus on the need for future self-directed learning and its rewards, provide the necessary knowledge and skills, and develop self-confidence in the ability to carry out the task.

5. *The individual is responsible for managing his or her own overseas experience.* Individuals are considered to be capable of making rational decisions and therefore are answerable for their behavior. In turn, the Navy accepts responsibility for providing the accurate, timely information and support needed by the individual to place the overseas transfer and adjustment process under his or her own control to the greatest extent possible. As Brislin, Dinges, and Fontaine (1981) observed, an accumulating body of behavioral science research indicates that social support systems can play several key roles in overseas training programs. The Navy has established a network of family service centers that perform these support functions.

Content and Sequencing. The framework upon which the Navy's ODSP rests is the overseas tour cycle. This cycle permits the Navy to determine where and what kind of intervention may be required to make a difference in the attitudes and performance of Navy members and families who are involved in a permanent change of station or being deployed in ships and air squadrons.

In some locations, ODSP has successfully initiated and maintained training and support at all points of this cycle, but reentry support still remains in the planning stage. To get the full "flavor" of the Navy's efforts, one should start at the beginning of the cycle.

Self/detailer selection. Individuals frequently need information to decide when the time is right to go overseas and which places to list on duty preference cards. ODSP offers two services at this time: (1) Overseas Living Conditions Fact Sheets, which succinctly describe overseas commands in terms of everything from health and housing to pets and passports, and (2) Overseas Transfer Information Service (OTIS), a telephone hotline that answers any questions people may have about an overseas transfer.

Suitability screening. Initial work by Yellen and Mumford (1975) attempted to develop selection strategies, but the researchers quickly realized that the emphasis should be on screening. Consequences of failure to fulfill overseas assignment were examined by Tucker and Schiller (1975) through a study of enlisted personnel who had terminated their overseas assignment early and returned to the United States for reasons that may have been detected through better screening. The results showed that a high percentage (6.05%) of enlisted personnel had to be returned early at a cost

115

to the Navy of more than six million dollars. As a result of this study, improved procedures were instituted. A five-year, follow-up study conducted by Benson, Hare, and Tucker (1980) yielded very positive results, indicating a vast reduction in the number of overseas failures. The percentage of early returns was reduced to 1.11 percent and the cost to 1.8 million dollars (Benson et al. 1980). Despite continued improvement in the reduction of early returns, overseas commands regard even this low percentage as intolerable. Consequently, ODSP continues to treat the area of suitability screening as an extremely important stage of the cycle.

Predeparture. This phase is very important in shaping the attitudes and expectations people take with them overseas. People are encouraged to collect information about the target country, to read newspaper or magazine articles, to seek out and talk with others who have been there, and to make decisions about a variety of things, such as what to take or leave here, how to arrange finances, what to do with the car. OTIS is of enormous help during this phase. Personnel are also put in touch with well-trained, highly motivated sponsors and are provided with well-organized Welcome Abroad packages.

Finally, predeparture overseas assignment workshops are being designed for families, and classes have been organized for high impact personnel and the overseas duty support coordinators aboard deploying ships. Various publications have been developed to support this phase, notably *Overseasmanship* (Naval Military Personnel Command 1983), a booklet filled with general information everyone in the Navy needs to know before going overseas; a seven-page OTIS checklist; port guides and language "computer" cards; and a series of age-graded Welcome Abroad booklets written by children for children. This is also a time when such information items as *Culturgrams* (1984) and Kohl's *Survival Kit for Overseas Living* (1979) are useful.

Transition. This short, intensive period is activated by the proximity of departure. It is often characterized by fatigue, action, and stress. The primary form of assistance to people in transition is to prepare them for it through the OTIS checklist and overseas assignment workshops.

In-country experience. In order to improve this important step in the cycle, ODSP initiated a "Standardization Project." The first step involved a study of current practices at overseas sites (Dodge 1984), followed by designing a core curriculum that incorporated the best of the present field programs, assumptions regarding adult learning, and current concepts in intercultural training. The results are program guidelines and a facilitator's guide that provide the information needed to conduct an effective, post-arrival overseas orientation program held at the overseas base. The standardized program contains both culture-general core curriculum and country-specific adaptation training.

ODSP coordinators at the overseas bases are required to meet the following objectives:

1. Provide a comfortable learning environment conducive to active participation.
2. Present information describing the base and area facilities and services.
3. Analyze the concept of culture as it applies to the self, cultural differences, and the process of adjusting to a new cultural environment.
4. Present facts describing the host country and culture.
5. Develop skills in communication, coping with adjustment, and interacting appropriately with host nationals.
6. Provide the basis for language learning.
7. Develop personal action plans that define individuals' roles and expectations for the overseas tour.
8. Provide a mechanism for evaluating the orientation program itself and the impact of the orientation on tour satisfaction.

The training has a general flow beginning with knowledge of self, knowledge of self as an American, awareness of cultural differences, communication and interpersonal skills, and ability to identify own role in the new culture. The facilitator's guide includes everything required for the instructional sessions, including objectives, procedures, timing, trainer's preparation, trainer's notes, handouts, newsprint designs, and logistics (a field trip is a requisite part of the training). The overall design has been tested and proved functional.

Mid-tour slump. This inelegant term refers to the difficult time when adjustment takes a downturn. Trivial problems become overwhelming, stress levels increase, and depression is common. The Navy identified this phenomenon using data from the family service center in Naples. They analyzed their calls and visits for assistance according to how long people had been in the country. The largest percentage of people who came in for help had been overseas 14–18 months. Naples is a 36-month assignment for married personnel. As yet, no specific programs exist that are designed to help people through this phase. The formal and informal social support networks become especially important here. Supervisors should be made aware of the effect this phase can have on attitudes and performance. Most people pull out of it, given time and patience.

Departure. Leaving an overseas assignment is different from a move within the continental United States. People need assistance in reaching closure on the overseas experience as well as preparation for returning home. A departure workshop in Keflavik and Sigonella has met with success but has not yet been implemented Navywide. A good departure workshop can take care of loose ends and get people ready to take on the task of reentry.

Reentry. According to Adler (1981), the readjustment cycle is shorter and more compressed than the overseas "culture shock" cycle, but no less intense or demanding. Reentry may be harder to cope with than the initial adjustment to a foreign culture. Going home is not easy, since people usually have changed in deep and subtle ways. As one can see in Austin's bibliography of cross-cultural reentry programs (1983), many workshops have been developed in the public and private sector to deal with reentry; however, the Navy has not yet tried reentry workshops. The vision of the overall program includes the design and implementation of reentry workshops at the Navy's family service centers in the United States.

Debriefing. The vision also includes systematic, selective debriefing. The overseas experience can be rich and rewarding, but the Navy loses an opportunity to capture important information about overseas tours by not debriefing members and families upon return. Building on the successes of the Canadian International Development Agency (Miner 1981), a debriefing process at the close of the cycle could be very beneficial for the Navy.

Conclusion

Recognizing the need for and providing organization-based support at each of the critical points in the overseas tour cycle underscores the philosophy that the Navy "takes care of its own." At its best, it also creates a professional force of members and families who know how to manage an overseas tour or foreign liberty and act as positive representatives of the United States while serving abroad.

The Navy regards its overseas orientation program as the entire configuration of the overseas experience, which is both a strength and a weakness. ODSP diversifies and, at times, overextends resources. But ODSP has also created a unified approach, at least from an organizational viewpoint. The ODSP practitioners can have a clear sense of where they fit into the cycle, and they can be trained toward the competency clusters constructed by McBer and Company (Mansfield 1982).

The Navy's approach is eclectic: it chooses what appears to be best from diverse sources, systems, and styles. It applies a multimedia and multimethod approach throughout the overseas tour cycle for each individual, family, or group with whom contact is made. An important priority for its future is filling gaps in the cycle.

Global organizations historically have a rather poor track record of working together. The cyclical framework of the Navy's program perhaps captures a core commonality for all organizational programs. By respecting the parallels in the experience of individuals transferring overseas, organizations can use these intervention points as a starting place for meaningful collaboration with each other. By treating a fairly wide range of situations as equivalent because of their timing, more complex and possibly better collaborative efforts may result in breakthroughs in overseas orientation.

References

Adler, Nancy J. 1981. Re-entry: Managing cross-cultural transitions. *Group and Organization Studies* 6(3):341–356.

Austin, Clyde N. 1983. *Cross-cultural re-entry: An annotated bibliography.* Abilene: Abilene Christian University Press.

Bedoian, James. 1980. *Study of the impact of the Navy's Overseas Duty Support Program as implemented within CINCUSNAVEUR.* (Report No: TM-(L)-7039/000/00). Washington, D.C.: Naval Military Personnel Command.

Benson, Phillip G., Gail B. Hare, and Michael F. Tucker. 1980. *Determination of the impact of revised screening system for overseas assignment.* (Report No. TM-(L)-6788/000/000). Washington, D.C.: Naval Military Personnel Command.

Bower, Eli M. 1967. American children and families in overseas communities. *American Journal of Orthopsychiatry* 37:787–796.

Brislin, Richard W. 1974. The establishment of re-entry/transition seminars for overseas sojourners. Paper presented at the Re-entry/Transition Workshop at Wingspread, Racine.

Brislin, Richard W., Norman G. Dinges, and Gary Fontaine. 1981. *The impact of cross-cultural training on overseas adjustment and performance: An integrative review.* (Report No. NR170-924). Washington, D.C.: Office of Naval Research.

Center for International and Area Studies. 1984. *Culturgrams.* Provo, Utah: Brigham Young University.

David, Henry P. and David Elkind. 1966. Family adaptation overseas. *Mental Hygiene* 50(1).

Dodge, Luanne. 1984. Description and analysis of current overseas orientation programs. Unpublished report. Washington, D.C.: Naval Military Personnel Command.

Fisher, Cynthia D., Garry Wilkins, and J. Eulberg. 1982. *Transfer transitions.* (Report No. TR-ONR-5). Washington, D.C.: Office of Naval Research.

Fritsch, J.F., J.L. Meinken, and W.C. Millerick. 1973. *Unobtrusive measures of intercultural relations: Results of a Puerto Rican data collection and evaluation report.* (Report No. TM-5100/000/00). Washington, D.C.: Naval Military Personnel Command.

Hayles, Robert. 1981, August. Discussant in S. Mumford (Chair), The intercultural experience: Impact on personnel and performance. Symposium conducted at the meeting of the American Psychological Association, Los Angeles.

Kohls, L. Robert. 1979. *Survival kit for overseas living.* Chicago: Intercultural Press.

Kohls, L. Robert and S. Howard. 1984. Benchmarks in the development of the field of intercultural communication in the United States. Unpublished manuscript.

Kraemer, Alfred J. 1981, August. The intercultural experience as a planned learning experience. In S. Mumford (Chair), The intercultural experience: Impact on personnel and performance. Symposium conducted at the meeting of the American Psychological Association, Los Angeles.

Mansfield, Richard S. 1982. *Advanced intercultural relations workshop design.* (McBer Report EG-91). Washington, D.C.: Naval Military Personnel Command.

Miner, Michael J. 1981. *A debriefing/re-entry process for external affairs.* Ottawa: Canadian International Development Agency.

Mumford, Sandra J. 1983. The cross-cultural experience: The program manager's perspective. In D. Landis and R.W. Brislin, eds., *Handbook of intercultural training, volume II: Issues in training methodology,* 82–99. New York: Pergamon.

Naval Military Personnel Command. 1984. *Overseas living conditions; information concerning.* (NAVMILPERSCOMINST 1720.1A). Washington, D.C.: Department of the Navy.

Naval Military Personnel Command. 1983. *Overseasmanship* (NAVPERS 15314, S/N 0500-LP-276-5320). Washington, D.C.: Department of the Navy.

Nice, D. Steven and Arnold L. Beck. 1978. *Cross-cultural adjustment of military families overseas.* (NHRC Report No. 78-58) San Diego: Naval Health Research Center.

Shirts, R. Garry. 1977. *Bafá Bafá: A cross cultural simulation.* Del Mar, CA: Simile II.

Sinaiko, H. Wallace. 1981, August. Discussant in S. Mumford (Chair), The intercultural experience: Impact on personnel and performance. Symposium conducted at the meeting of the American Psychological Association, Los Angeles.

Torbiörn, Ingemar. 1982. *Living abroad: Personnel adjustment and personal policy in the overseas setting.* Chichester: John Wiley & Sons.

Triandis, Harry C. 1981, August. Satisfaction with contact with another culture. In S. Mumford (Chair), The intercultural experience: Impact on personnel and performance. Symposium conducted at the meeting of the American Psychological Association, Los Angeles.

Tucker, Michael F. and John E. Schiller. 1975. *An assessment of the screening problem for overseas assignment in the U.S. Navy.* (Task Order No. 75/533). Washington, D.C.: Naval Military Personnel Command.

Yellen, Ted M.I. and Sandra J. Mumford. 1975. *The cross-cultural interaction inventory: Development of overseas criterion measures and items that differentiate between successful and unsuccessful adjusters.* (NPRDC Report No. TR 75-27). (NTIS AD-A009362).

16

New Data on U.S. Students Abroad: Implications for Orientation

Jolene Koester

Students constitute an important element in the exchange of persons across national boundaries. Brown (1983) estimates that some 750,000 U.S. students work, travel, or study abroad per year, and the Institute of International Education (1984) indicates that 338,890 students from other countries studied in the United States in 1983–84. These students are often motivated by an implicit faith that, in the words of J. William Fulbright, "what we must all try to acquire through education, and especially through international education, is some degree of perception and perspective about the various peoples of the world..." (Fulbright 1983).

Program administrators support orientation and training of sojourners as a means to achieve the goals Fulbright described. Advances in the conceptualization and research of orientation issues continually help us better understand the role orientation plays in the international experience. Yet, orientation planning for U.S. college students has often taken place without a base of information about students and what they do on their international sojourns. *Profile of the U.S. Student Abroad* (Koester 1985), a large-scale survey, has important implications for orientation programs.

Overview of the Research Project

The research culminating in this publication began in 1983, when the Council on International Educational Exchange (CIEE) started to use the International Student Identity Card (ISIC) to collect information on U.S. students who go abroad. The ISIC, available globally to students, is sold in the United States under the supervision of the council. CIEE's publication *The Student Travel Catalog* contains an application for the ISIC. Beginning in 1982–83, this application included a questionnaire to collect demographic, attitudinal, and descriptive information on U.S. students who study, travel, and work abroad.

The first set of questionnaire items was designed to answer the question, Who is the student who participates in international experiences. The

121

second set of items attempted to provide a description of the student's intended international experience. The third cluster of questions addressed motivational and behavioral issues. Finally, students with prior international experiences were asked for a self-assessment of the impact of that experience.

The results reported in this chapter are based on responses of approximately 5,900 students who purchased the ISIC, primarily by mail, through the council's New York office. Because these applications originate all over the country, the data set is heterogeneous; nevertheless, the findings may not fully represent all U.S. students traveling abroad. Not all applicants for the ISIC fill out the questionnaire, and those who do may have a special interest in international education. Also, the ISIC is more visible and popular among travelers to European destinations. Finally, variations in administering the questionnaire influence the overall reliability, validity, and generalizability of the results.

Still, the description that results from these data represents an exciting portrait of the traveling U.S. student, one that can serve to direct orientation efforts for U.S. students going abroad. *Profile of the U.S. Student Abroad* contains a complete description of the study and its methodology as well as its results.

Selected Research Results

Respondents provided information on a number of questions relevant to orientation. This included a description of their proposed international experience, its length, their personal goals, major concerns, and the sources of influence that sharpened their interest in international sojourn. This information, coupled with data on their majors, year in school, and language facility, suggests directions for orientation activities.

Orientation is defined in the broadest sense as including curricular offerings, extended extra-curricular programs, and one-time events, ranging from educational to training programs (Gudykunst and Hammer 1983). The results of the study imply that orientation planners must utilize a full range of alternatives to adequately meet the orientation needs of students.

Respondents ranked (from one to three) up to three descriptors of the nature of their intended international experience. The summary of respondent choices is presented in Table 1. A significant number of these respondents participated in a program sponsored by a U.S. educational in-stitution. The high ranking of educational travel among the three descriptors implies that students are traveling internationally because of a perceived educational objective. Orientation programs should capitalize on this and include material related to cultures and cultural interaction.

Data on the students' academic years and fields of study confirm and challenge some of the traditional wisdom about U.S. students who travel.

TABLE 1
Type of International Experience Planned
(In Percentages)

	Ranked First Choice	Ranked Second Choice	Ranked Third Choice	Total
Program sponsored by U.S. educational institution	29	6	5	15
Direct enrollment in foreign institution/program	5	3	2	4
Independent study abroad	7	8	10	8
Paid work	4	4	4	4
Voluntary work	1	2	3	2
Visit/live with family/friends	9	14	17	13
Travel with family/friends	18	19	20	19
Educational travel	22	41	27	30
Other	5	3	12	6
	100%	100%	100%	100%
N =	5743	5130	4078	14,951

While 22 percent were in the third year post-high-school, 18 percent and 21 percent were in the fourth and fifth year post-high-school. Only six percent were in the first year post-high-school and 14 percent in the second. High school students constituted 20 percent. This distribution within the college career takes on a slightly different meaning when cross-tabulated with students' descriptions of their types of intended international experiences, as Table 2 indicates.

These results indicate that students in a program sponsored by a U.S. educational institution who enrolled in a foreign institution or studied independently were concentrated in the third year post-high-school. The distribution of students engaging in work-related activities was highest in the fourth and fifth post-high-school years. For those traveling or living with family or friends, the distribution was relatively even for all years except the first year post-high-school. Such data suggest programs designed for students planning international sojourns should target different populations for different orientations. For example, advanced undergraduate students should be the target for courses in intercultural relations offered by departments of communication, anthropology, and education.

Students also indicated their fields of study. A large proportion came from foreign language majors (12%) and other liberal arts (21%). But, significantly, 10 percent were in engineering or the physical sciences, and

123

TABLE 2
YEAR IN SCHOOL BY FIRST CHOICE TYPE OF EXPERIENCE

First Choice— Type of Experience	High School	1st Year Post HS	2nd Year Post HS	3rd Year Post HS	4th Year Post HS	5th Year Post HS	N =
Program sponsored by U.S. educational institution	14	5	17	37	13	15 = 100%	1657
Direct enrollment in foreign institution	15	4	16	28	14	24	293
Independent study	9	6	17	22	18	27	381
Paid work	3	10	12	16	27	33	223
Volunteer work	13	3	15	18	19	34	80
Visit/live with family/friends	30	8	12	12	14	23	512
Travel with family/friends	20	5	9	12	25	28	993
Educational travel	22	6	15	20	20	18	1221
Other	42	5	10	11	13	19	264

13 percent were in business. The first result suggests the use of the foreign language classroom as the context for orientation programs. The merging of substantive orientation material with foreign language instruction would capitalize on the numbers of foreign language majors seeking international experiences. This would be particularly useful and functional in the more advanced language courses. Intercultural communication scholars and international program administrators need to work with foreign language faculty to develop special units on intercultural communication and cultural preparation to include in foreign language courses.

The significant number of engineering, physical science, and business students going abroad, however, suggests a need to develop and target orientation programs to these populations. Business students, for example, would require programs that highlight the role of cultural differences in knowledge and practice of business activities. Because these student groups are not traditionally identified as receptive to study, travel, and work abroad activities, special efforts may be necessary to reach them in promoting campus orientation activities.

Regarding the length of the trips, most students (49%) were traveling for one to three months. Fourteen percent were traveling less than one month. Three-to-six and six-to-twelve months were selected by 17 percent of the students. Only four percent were planning a trip of more than one year. Even when length of trip is cross-tabulated with type of experience, the one-to-three-month time frame was selected most often by students participating in almost all types of experiences. (Those directly enrolling in a foreign institution selected six-to-twelve-month experiences at 35 percent, compared to 31 percent selecting the one-to-three-month experience.) This, too, has interesting implications for predeparture training. It suggests that orientation programs offered to shorter-trip students should be fairly compact with respect to time and content, since they would probably not commit themselves to long programs.

Several other questions on the survey are particularly germane to the content and mechanics of orientation programs. By ranking three choices, applicants indicated their major concerns about the trip and their personal goals (See Table 3).

Having enough money is a concern to students participating in all types of experiences, as is language proficiency. Uneasiness about language and cultural adjustment are important for those participating in U.S. educational institution-sponsored programs. Intercultural communication educators and study-travel education personnel need to work with language instructors to develop language training modules for orientation. These could improve (or even introduce) language skills while simultaneously teaching cultural awareness and intercultural interaction skills. For example, a language exercise related to conversational appropriateness in ritualistic social situations could at the same time highlight the culture's values as revealed in interaction.

Respondents selected up to three personal goals for their sojourn experience. The striking aspect of this information (presented in Table 4), is the degree to which students selected an educational objective for their travels. Almost half of those on programs sponsored by U.S. educational institutions indicated they were attempting to add a new dimension to their schooling; another 22 percent wanted to improve their foreign language ability. Even among those students who planned to visit, live, or travel with family or friends, about 50 percent indicated some kind of educational objective. Orientation planners are therefore challenged to develop alternatives to capitalize on this expressed interest. Our students are saying they want to learn about the countries and cultures they are visiting; it is up to us to respond to their interests with creative programming.

Recommendations for Orientation of U.S. Students Going Abroad

Based on these descriptions of U.S. students who study, travel, and work abroad, several recommendations can be made to improve orientation efforts.

125

TABLE 3

TYPE OF EXPERIENCE BY MAJOR CONCERN

	Housing	Food	Language	Adjustment	Having Sufficient Money	Meeting People	Health	Political Unrest	Home Sickness	Other 2 = 100%	N =
Program sponsored by U.S. educational institution	9	2	28	19	25	10	2	1	1	2	1595
Direct enrollment in foreign institution	16	1	23	17	20	14	0	1	3	4	278
Independent study	14	3	22	14	26	11	2	3	1	4	370
Paid work	15	3	9	8	34	14	3	1	4	8	214
Voluntary work	19	3	18	14	28	11	0	0	0	7	72
Visit/live with family/friends	12	2	21	11	30	15	3	1	3	3	486
Travel with family/friends	21	3	20	7	29	14	2	1	1	2	952
Educational travel	14	2	23	14	26	12	3	2	1	3	1199
Other	13	1	29	15	20	11	1	2	3	7	261

TABLE 4
TYPE OF EXPERIENCE BY MAJOR PERSONAL GOAL

	Add New Dimension Schooling	Improve Foreign Language	Improve Knowledge Countries	Have Fun	Meet People	Changes	Improve Self-Confidence	Gain Independence	Other
Program sponsored by U.S. educational institution	48	22	12	5	3	4	3	3	2 = 100%
Direct enrollment in foreign institution	39	32	11	5	1	4	3	3	2
Independent study	42	22	16	4	3	3	4	3	3
Paid work	17	15	24	13	6	5	5	9	6
Voluntary work	37	16	20	8	5	3	0	4	7
Visit/live with family/friends	16	15	21	26	10	3	2	3	4
Travel with family/friends	15	5	28	38	5	4	2	3	1
Educational travel	31	14	25	11	6	4	3	5	1
Other	11	14	22	18	9	8	3	5	10

127

1. *The foreign language classroom should be utilized as a vehicle for orientation.* Both the large numbers of foreign language majors on international sojourns and the inherent relationship between language learning and culture learning point to the language classroom as a locus for orientation. Culture-learning orientation should be done as a regular part of classroom language instruction. While the number of students in a given language class planning an immediate overseas trip may be small, the ISIC data suggest many will make that sojourn at a later date.

2. *Language training outside of regular curricular offerings should be made available to students embarking on visits to foreign countries.* Students engaging in all types of sojourns expressed great concern about language. Therefore, international education administrators should develop alternate ways to improve language skills for students who are not language majors. A willingness to provide what might be deemed rather superficial language training, such as conversational routines or the use of a bilingual dictionary, seems appropriate to meet quite a few of these students' needs. As a side benefit, students otherwise afraid of learning languages might discover a new enthusiasm for language learning. This approach to language learning has generally received little support on the college campus. It is time to re-evaluate attitudes and adjust programming decisions with respect to language training for non-language majors.

3. *Efforts and resources should be directed at developing orientation offerings for students who travel abroad for short periods on programs not sponsored by U.S. educational institutions.* International education administrators generally devote the bulk of human and monetary resources to orientation for students in traditional study-abroad activities. The ISIC survey results challenge that choice. Significant numbers of U.S. students choose other types of activities, but with specific educational objectives in mind. By ignoring this group or minimizing their significance, an important means of achieving the overall objectives of international exchange is being overlooked. While it is naturally more difficult to plan orientation programs for students who are not involved in a formal campus program, one-time programs on a wide range of topics should be developed.

Creative program development is also needed for the significant number of students planning one-to-three-month sojourns. The incorporation of written materials may be necessary to accommodate time constraints. In the past this group, too, has been neglected, and another chance to encourage intercultural empathy and tolerance overlooked.

4. *Orientation programs should be developed for students in professionally and/or scientifically oriented fields.* The ISIC survey demonstrates that a large number of students from fields not traditionally associated with study and travel abroad do pursue the international option. Orientation activities located within these departments and colleges,

perhaps associated with regular curricular offerings or based within the fields of study (as an orientation session on the mechanics of setting up engineering projects in different parts of the world), should be favorably received.

5. *International program administrators, foreign language educators, and intercultural relations specialists need to work together to develop orientation programs.* College and university structures that militate against cooperative efforts between individuals from different administrative and teaching units must be overcome to provide orientation for the wide variety of U.S. students traveling internationally. One-time grant support should be sought to bring together individuals from different parts of the campus to develop orientation modules (both for programs conducted in person and those conducted only through distribution of written materials) that can be used in the kinds of orientation activities recommended above.

6. *More attention should be paid to the development of orientation programs and material that is culture-general.* Almost half the students filling out the ISIC questionnaire have had at least one international travel experience. International travel, study, and work abroad is obviously not a "once in a lifetime" experience. It is important, then, to provide the conceptual and interactional skills that function in any cultural setting.

Conclusion

Any attempt to implement these recommendations will require the commitment of human and fiscal resources — commodities often in short supply on our campuses. Nevertheless, the description of U.S. students emerging from the survey included in the International Student Identity Card implies a need to re-evaluate campus orientation activities to ensure that the potential of all international exchanges is developed.

References

Brown, M. Archer. 1983. U.S. students abroad. In Hugh Jenkins and Associates, eds., *Educating students from other nations.* San Francisco: Jossey-Bass.

Fulbright, J. William. 1983. Address to the annual meeting of the Council on International Educational Exchange, Washington D.C.

Gudykunst, William B. and Mitchell R. Hammer. 1983. Basic training design: Approaches to intercultural training. In Dan Landis and Richard Brislin, eds., *Handbook of intercultural training, volume I: Issues in theory and design.* New York: Pergamon.

Koester, Jolene. 1985. *Profile of the U.S. student abroad.* New York: Council on International Educational Exchange.

Institute for International Education. 1984. *Open doors.* New York: IIE.

PART TWO
Blending Culture, Learning, and the Disciplines

17

Concepts and Theories of Culture Learning

Josef A. Mestenhauser

In Part II we will examine in detail the concepts and theories used by practitioners as described in Part I. Not all of the authors identified these theories explicitly; we here translate what they have written into a theoretical framework, based on the literature dealing with cross-cultural orientation. Following is an alphabetical listing of these concepts and theories, with brief identification and references to examples in the preceding chapters.

actuation—satisfaction of basic human needs, organized in hierarchies (based on writings of Maslow [1954]). Cited explicitly by Soquet as a theoretical foundation of the Experiment in International Living's orientation programs; used by EIL for sequencing of materials and learning. Implied strongly by Mumford Fowler in connection with services available for transporting bodies but not emotions, people, and needs.

adjustment—the process of seeking equilibrium that has been upset by circumstances; assumes stress, transition, uncertainty, misunderstandings, communication, fear, etc. Mentioned by virtually every author describing objectives of orientation.

algorithms—organized learning experience, such as the body of knowledge of a discipline; also assumes learning by experience, but experience is "given" by the discipline (e.g., organized field trip, laboratory). Referred to by Clarke in connection with faculty participation in an orientation retreat.

analogy—method of comparison. Many examples through the text (e.g., assumptions that a classroom in the United States is like a classroom in the home country, or vice versa; that reentry is like any other transition in life).

analysis—process of thinking involving several intellectual skills (e.g., critical thinking, doubting authority, independent thinking, identification of parts of a whole). Basic assumption in all orientation program descriptions that teach study skills; basic advice given to U.S. students for study abroad.

andragogy—adult motivation theory (based on Knowles [1980]) that assumes people have an intrinsic motivation to be competent, effective, and self-determining to the extent of their abilities, achieve these goals with the drive to learn from practical experiences—depending on what they need to know at any particular stage of their psychological development—and then apply their knowledge to new situations. The intellectual basis of EIL programs as cited by Soquet.

attributions—a concept of social and self-perception: ascribing to others and self qualities based on perceptions and stereotypes in order to understand or explain complex behavior and motives. According to Rosenquist Watts, the concept least-known by U.S. orientation practitioners; key concept in cross-cultural training in Triandis, Brislin; common method in debriefing of *Bafá Bafá* simulation game.

cognitive dissonance—a concept of decision-making based on choosing among equally attractive alternatives that causes inner conflict; assumed in counseling approaches to orientation, but not normally associated with the possibility that the emphasis on individual responsibility and making choices in the United States may itself be a cause of such conflict. It may be a critical factor in initiating U.S.-international student interpersonal relations. According to Steglitz, little known or used by orientation practitioners.

cognitive distortion—treating unrelatable variables as if they were related. Example in Mumford Fowler of Vietnamese who thought that cross-culturally trained Marines came from another part of the United States.

comparative thinking—method of comparing parts to parts and to wholes. Many examples used by Sarles in interpreting the United States to Fulbright scholars.

conformity—social psychological influence resulting from relationships between majorities and minorities. In Byrd as fear of "indoctrination"; in O'Driscoll as the purpose of early orientation—to give incoming foreign students fair competitive advantages with U.S. students.

culture contact—interaction between a significant number of people from two cultures over time. Implicit in all orientation programs urging students to use local resources and natives as sources of information; assumed in all international education programs; has consequences to other concepts, e.g., the "third culture" (Useem 1963).

culture fatigue—results from prolonged living in another culture. According to Nicholson, mitigation requires all-pervasive cross-cultural training component and strong inner personal resources; if not dealt with, it can lead to culture shock and failure of assignment. It may be the unconscious source of foreign student clubs' desires and efforts to orient students from their countries themselves.

culture-general method of studying any culture by understanding variations of general cultural principles. Most common method in foreign student orientation, but also used in U.S. orientation (in Clarke, Felsing).

culture shock — disequilibrium caused by encounter with other cultures. Listed by Rosenquist Watts as the best-known concept in U.S. student orientation, by Steglitz as the best known in foreign student orientation.

culture-specific — method of studying and teaching a single culture or specific aspects of specific cultures, e.g., marketing. Felsing; Clarke; Nicholson in connection with in-country orientation for Peace Corps.

decision-making — resolving problems and acting on resolution; assumed in most foreign student "information"-model orientations (e.g., "give them basic information so that they can make their own decisions"). Handled cross-culturally by Sarles.

deductive — method of thinking from general principles, common in countries without Anglo-Saxon tradition. Assumed by most foreign student study-skill programs.

dependency — relationship of dominance by one party. In Steglitz, a common fear of orientation organizers is that orientation will produce dependency on "experts"; Soquet shows a strong emphasis in EIL training on producing independence and self-reliance.

differentiation — intellectual skill of identifying parts of a whole and distinguishing them from each other and from the whole. Strong emphasis by Baker; Sarles provides many examples in connection with U.S. culture.

double classification — retaining information in two cognitive categories. Examples are assumed in programs that include a home-stay (e.g., the concept of "family" in home and host culture).

education shock — disequilibrium based on encounter with a different educational system and method of instruction. Assumed in all study-skill programs for foreign students and foreign teaching assistants.

emic and *etic* — emic is the study of unique features of cultures, etic is the study of common features of cultures; training based on seeing another culture from the point of view of "insiders" (emic) as well as "outsiders" (etic). Assumed in Clarke, Baker, and Gamboa; explicit in Sarles.

epistemic motivation — self-motivation based on activity that generates greater motivation to perform that activity. Explicitly used in Clarke as the excitement of study abroad that creates desire for more.

equal status — hypothesis (based on Amir [1969]) that satisfactory interpersonal relationships between people of different cultures depends on equal status. Assumed in most programs, explicit in Mumford Fowler as the need to treat foreigners with dignity and acceptance.

ethnocentrism — seeing one's own culture as the center of the universe, assumed to be the major problem for all sojourners; if not changed causes negative attributions. Explicit in Clarke; see also Sarles.

expectations—variable determining the severity of culture shock. Implicit in all orientation programs that prepare publications for sojourners prior to departure; assumed by organizers who include culture shock in the content of programs.

field theory—an interdisciplinary social psychological theory (based on Lewin [1951]) that learning is based on the need to abstract knowledge from the entire field of activity. Defined in Nicholson; used in Soquet as the basis of observation training in the host country.

heuristic—randomly acquired experience as a basis of learning. Assumed in all experiential learning approaches (e.g., EIL, Peace Corps).

holistic—the ability to perceive the universe and its component parts; similar to but not to be equated with Gestalt. Assumed in Clarke's discussion of "unpredictable" experiences, and in Gamboa as foreign students' reaction toward experiential strategies.

ideal type—method of comparison by constructing a type against which to measure reality; a research method. Simulation games are based on this method.

imitation—uncritical acceptance of other people's ideas or solutions; leads to dependency. Assumed to be a problem in A.I.D.-based orientation programs described by Cadman.

inductive—method of thinking and reasoning, deriving general principles from empirical observations; basis of critical thinking and analytical abilities. Implicit in all programs of study skills.

influence—power relationship. Basis of all modules dealing with critical and independent thinking; common in situations of anxiety and uncertainty. In Byrd, the fear of indoctrination.

integration—thinking simultaneously of several variables and their relationships; also the relationship between people and social systems. A basic strategy in liberal studies programs; implicit in Clarke.

Johari window—grid showing relationships of people and their knowledge of each other, or lack of it (based on Luft [1969]). Assumed in most information-based orientation programs, i.e. that sojourners do not know enough. Explicit in Byrd, Felsing; interesting example in Clarke, that students want more knowledge after they return home.

learning-to-learn—understanding the process of how knowledge accumulates. Basis of EIL and Peace Corps programs.

mainstreaming—a concept of majority-minority relations that requires functioning in a society on its own terms. All adjustment-oriented programs assume mainstreaming. Explicit in O'Driscoll; implicit in all advice given to newcomers about how to identify and use "exceptions" from rules.

modeling—designing a hypothetical type as part of experimental thinking. Evidenced where simulations and role plays are used.

perceptions—a body of beliefs and process of thinking that permits people to understand how their environment functions with respect to themselves. Example of a common U.S. perception in Sarles: opposing views are considered equivalent based on a perception of fairness (Singer 1987).

process learning—understanding how cognitive processes function. All skill training in cross-cultural communication is process-oriented. See Byrd, Soquet, Baker.

product learning—accumulating a quantum of knowledge. Examples in Clarke of academic subject matter based on disciplines (e.g., history, geography.)

self-motivation—ability to energize one's self. Assumed in EIL and Soquet; explicit in Clarke.

snapshot picture—an arrested and unchanging perception of other cultures based on experience or an understanding of history. Assumed in reentry programs.

social change—pattern of growth in people and institutions over time. Examples in Sarles: the need to convey an understanding of trends based on historical and cultural patterns, to prevent the snapshot picture of another culture.

sociotyping—categorizing people by social status rather than national origin. Presumed to be a step away from ethnocentrism and stereotyping. Implicit in Baker.

stages of cognitive development—based on several psychological developmental theories: learning occurs in stages according to age, from concrete to abstract reasoning. Implicit in Soquet; explicit in Bennett (1986b)

stress and transition—emotional or behavioral disequilibrium stemming from changes in personal life and relationships. Assumed in every counseling-based orientation program. Explicit in Mumford Fowler.

transfer of learning—ability to use knowledge obtained in one setting in another. See Cadman in connection with A.I.D.'s interest in maximizing transfer-of-technology potential through enrichment programs.

U-curve—hypothetical pattern of adjustment to another culture in several stages: observing, fighting the system, coming to terms, reentering home culture. Steglitz and Rosenquist Watts identified it as the most commonly known and used concept.

values—system of culturally acquired beliefs and habits that permit individuals and institutions to maintain a comprehensive cultural identity. Dominant variable in culture-learning approaches, simulations, case studies, lectures about other cultures, and language training.

We must become familiar with how these concepts relate to orientation. Readers may have noticed that the practitioners in Part I referred to them only sparingly; all of these concepts were in use, however, either implicity or explicitly.

The concepts appear to fall into two broad categories: "culture" and "cognitive processes." Some—like emic, etic, inductive, deductive—can fit in both categories, and thus overlap or intersect with each other.

Without some organization and order, these concepts become confusing and overwhelming. However, they do relate to each other in a variety of ways. Some relate on the basis of similarity or difference, such as comparative thinking, emic and etic, and education shock. Much of cross-cultural learning is based on assumptions of how we understand ourselves in relationship to others. Now add ethnocentrism to this relationship and it might change from lineal to hierarchical if the ethnocentrically-behaving persons think their culture is superior to others. This would, of course, invalidate the equal status hypothesis and render it inoperative.

Analytical thinking could also produce hierarchical relationships, either because some variables lead one from another, or because the choice of analytical categories make comparisons culture-bound and ethnocentric. Still other relationships are based on inferential contingency, such as the relationship between expectations and culture shock: if expectations are too high and out of touch with reality, then culture shock is likely to occur, and it is likely to be severe.

There are many other relationships, and relationships between relationships, that we cannot pursue here. However, one that does deserve attention here is the sequential relationship, such as in the U-curve concept. For example, if culture shock is overcome and the conditions for a solution identified, then in time the individual may move into another stage on the curve and "adjust" functionally. Time sequences are especially important to all explanations that require historical analysis, to theories of social change and cognitive development, and to actuation concepts.

Now let us add another dimension to these concepts. Some have either a positive or negative "loading," while others are neutral. The loading can depend on the values held in our field as a whole; others, such as culture shock or mainstreaming, may be positive for some of us and negative for others.

If we had the inclination, skill, and space, we could construct a tree structure of these concepts after they were carefully described, defined, and explained (this would be a cross-cultural task of great magnitude in itself). Such a structure would yield practical information, such as how to sequence orientation materials and how to structure training programs. Very likely, as Donald suggests (1985), it would cluster the concepts, with a few central concepts fanning out into others like a web. This is how social science concepts generally relate to each other. An example might be "socialization," a concept common to several social sciences, one from which other concepts flow. Natural science and engineering concepts, however, generally resemble building blocks that fit neatly in hierarchical patterns. This may explain why we have difficulty explaining our concepts to our colleagues in the sciences.

The Role of Culture in Orientation

Learning about other cultures is logically one of the most dominant concerns of all orientation programs. However, the exact role that culture plays in study abroad is as ambivalent as its perception in the many academic disciplines on which we as professionals draw, the disciplines our students study here and abroad. Culture is the sole focus of anthropology, but it plays a less prominent role in other fields. Many social and behavioral sciences, including psychology and business administration, treat culture as an independent variable, and at times ascribe to it a negative loading, as if culture were something one could blame when business does not go smoothly. A similar range of views and variety of meanings prevail in orientation programs.

Some practitioners, such as Clarke at a liberal arts college, consider knowledge of another culture part of a liberal education and a meta-goal of education, accepted and reinforced by the teaching faculty and administration. Others think of culture as a set of prescriptions that a sojourner must know in order to function in other countries. Hanvey (1976), in describing varieties of cross-cultural "sophistications," suggested that the most common one is a simple set of "do's and don't's" that do not require "culture sharing" but do permit the majority of sojourners to function effectively in other cultures. Others represented in this volume (Sarles, Felsing) assume that understanding other cultures can occur only when people understand their own. This view is reinforced by Stewart (1972), who developed an entire teaching strategy based on the "American-Contrast American" model. In general, most practitioners in international education and cross-cultural scholarship have borrowed a great deal from the social sciences and molded it with their daily experiences into workable assumptions and concepts about culture that they can use in their jobs.

Even as we treat culture as a subject matter of orientation, it is at work in every facet of our programs. All the players in an orientation program have been infused by their separate cultures with values that determine their attitudes, behaviors, and teaching and learning styles and abilities. Here we will highlight only three aspects of culture learning that do not receive adequate attention in either theory or practice but are treated, if sparingly, in this volume: first, the role of culture as a conformi-

139

ty agent; second, which cultural principles—specific to one country or general to all—should be included in orientation; and third, how and when we know that we know about our own and other cultures.

Culture, Influence, and Conformity. The counseling paradigm that supports many orientation programs is based on the premise that individuals need services and assistance to deal with stress from cross-cultural relations. In this schema, culture itself is treated narrowly, in terms of values and value conflicts. The very fact that we have orientation programs acknowledges that we consider culture to be a force that causes pressure on people under which they must adjust. Similarly, the very issue of adjustment begs a series of questions related to influence and conformity, broader issues of culture than of values; for example, "Adjustment to what?", "How much adjustment?","Who must do the adjusting?", "What is the consequence of not adjusting?", and "What is the psychological and cultural cost of adjusting?". We have yet another meaning of culture in our orientation programs. Few of us hide our expectation that educational exchanges will lead to friendly attitudes and future relations between countries as a result of participants learning enough about their host-country cultures to develop appreciation for them. Yet we put pressure on those who return from study abroad if they appear to have "gone native" and thus become "too influenced" by the other culture.

For these and other reasons to be explored in this section, we prefer to use the broader definition of culture provided by Hofstede (1984). He showed culture to be an independent variable that "programs" not only people's values, but such things as perceptions, attitudes, ideas about power, influence, conformity, leadership, responsibility, trust and mistrust, division of labor, and organization of knowledge, as well as a sense for dealing with uncertainties and insecurities.

Several of our authors understood culture's role this way. Clarke, for example, identified receptivity to attitude changes as a primary objective of the orientation retreat, recognizing that the major problem for U.S. students is inappropriate attitudes rather than lack of knowledge. Similarly, Felsing dealt with the expectation that U.S. students abroad be perceived as representatives of their entire culture, contrary to the highly individualistic U.S. value system. Byrd commented that the ESL teacher is a minority of one among a majority of foreign students. Incoming foreign students often tell us of promising their parents they will not "change" while in the United States. Practitioners report difficulties explaining the concept of individual responsibility to Japanese or Indonesians, in whose cultures belonging and conformity are highly valued while individualism is equated with selfishness. But despite occasional references to these concepts, orientation programs generally do not sufficiently recognize such cultural manifestations as influence, power, authority, or conformity.

As orientation organizers, we are perceived by our incoming foreign student clientele as having influence. In this role, we commonly tell them to use all available campus services and resources. But what they hear instead may be quite different. "Mainstreaming" may be understood to induce conformity to majority (U.S.) norms. Students from highly "collectivistic" cultures, to use Hofstede's term (1984), might easily perceive an orientation program as an agent of conformity to our culture, causing loss of their own cultural identities. We may also spend an inordinate amount of time and effort in orientation programs on rules and regulations—U.S. government rules, university rules, and, yes, international office rules. Hofstede described rule-making and religious revival as culturally influenced responses to uncertainty. In other cultures the response to uncertainty may be very different, such as withdrawal. Withdrawal is in fact the response of many foreign students to the complex rules that in turn heighten their anxieties and uncertainties in the United States.

We might not think about influence and conformity when selecting resource persons for international student orientation, but the issue is there. Paige (1986) noted an interesting difference of opinion. Some advocate using volunteer veteran foreign students (Saltzman 1986), and others such as Westwood, Lawrence, and McBlane (1986) urge that effective orientation for international students be provided by host-country student volunteers. Several authors represented in this volume include both U.S. and foreign students as orientation resources. This is indeed an issue of some conceptual and practical consequence. First, there may be a real difference in their perspectives about major emphases of orientation. People learn about their own country differently from the way they learn about other cultures, so orientation using host-country and foreign resource persons may have a different outcome depending on such things as how the resources themselves perceive the relationship between the host country and other countries, and whether they think in an "emic" or "etic" way about their own problems or experiences. Clinical experience shows that selected veteran foreign and returned U.S. students, orienting others of their own nationality, have greater ability to understand and deal with complexity and can provide comparative insights and correctives of stereotypes.

On the other hand, using Americans to orient foreign students or vice versa suggests that there is a perceived difference in the quality and accuracy of these resource persons according to their nationality. For example, there are strong social-psychological pressures to doubt that foreign students can be effective educators and learning resources for U.S. students. Similarly, foreign students often organize their own orientation on the grounds that they know best what to tell newcomers about

141

Americans. When this occurs, we can be sure that ethnocentrism is at work. It does not occur only on campuses in relation to educational exchanges: for instance, Ezra Vogel's (1979) suggestion that Americans have a few things to learn from the Japanese was initially treated with a great deal of hostility and suspicion.

Hanvey (1976) concluded that ethnocentrism, with all its implications, is actually a natural state for most people, the result of one's upbringing and experiences. Yet, as we well know, ethnocentrism is not a simple attitude to treat. If unchecked it causes dangerous cognitive distortions that are difficult to correct and can have serious consequences. It was recently diagnosed as a cause of growing problems with creativity and productivity in U.S. engineering. A report by the National Academy of Engineering (1987) cited the "reluctance or inability of U.S. firms to take advantage of technical information generated elsewhere" as one of the "fundamental shifts in dominant technologies":

> A long term perspective is usually required to benefit from cooperation with foreign institutions, and many organizations are not willing to take such a view and make the necessary up-front investment. U.S. industrial success earlier in this century has led to an attitude of superiority and prejudice against the need to learn what the rest of the world is doing. There is a reluctance to recognize that the immediate post-World War II period of U.S. economic dominance has come to an end. A bias against using what is "not invented here" is embedded in many organizational cultures; many are disinclined to look outside established networks for knowledge and partners. Foreign travel is viewed intrinsically as a waste of time and money by some company and university administrators. (National Academy of Engineering 1987)

A few years ago, this bias appeared in U.S. students taking a course that relied heavily on international students from Turkey, Nigeria, and Thailand as resources. These countries were all known for their friendly policies toward the United States, and the international student resources were so enthusiastic about their role that they wrote to their home countries for literature in English about various aspects of development (the focus of the course). The literature was placed on reserve in the library, and the American students were repeatedly encouraged to read and compare it with similar perspectives in U.S. literature on the same subject. At the end of the term not one student had done so; they obviously preferred the familiar and presumably more credible information published in the United States.

As we have seen, most orientation programs appear to take influence, conformity, and perceptions for granted and concentrate on individuals' adjustment to these forces. The most common medium used to teach about culture is the *Bafá Bafá* simulation game, which has been shown to effectively demonstrate the concepts of values and adjustment. Less commonly used but more effective is the Star Power simulation game, more appropriate for conveying broader cultural concepts, including power, influence, conformity, and majority-minority relations. It highlights several difficult pedagogical issues, including the impact of study abroad on individuals; how to retain one's individual or cultural identity; possible over emphasis on adjustment, which heightens the anxieties an orientation program is supposed to remove; and real and perceived power and influence in international educational exchanges. This last issue can determine how students are motivated to learn about other cultures, how they view mainstreaming, and how they utilize available resources for an enrichment program.

One of the little-known but conceptually rich and useful concepts on conformity has been developed by Moscovici (1976). It holds that conformity and influence are present in all relationships between majorities and minorities, and that such influence is mutual and reciprocal rather than one-sided and unidirectional. Students studying in other countries often feel helpless and overwhelmed by the host culture, but they would be comforted by application of Moscovici's theories, which hold that they have an equal influence on host-country educators. The very need to organize orientation programs in which we interpret and explain ourselves to the foreign student, for example, is evidence of such influence. Similarly, students exercise a great deal of influence on orientation leaders simply by their presence or absence. To cite another example, foreign students influence U.S. students in decisions to study abroad as much as faculty members do (Koester 1987).

Culture-General and Culture-Specific. Culture plays a more tangible role in the focus of orientation programs. The most common models of culture learning are based on Kluckhohn's cultural universals (1961), which have been formatted into the "culture general" approach, emphasizing values. The early writings (Brislin & Pedersen 1976) followed this style, treating orientation as a generic process, regardless of client nationalities. Other scholars of cross-cultural communication (Howell 1977; Broome 1978) placed culture learning squarely into the single culture, "culture-specific" category. Sarles and Kohls (1988 forthcoming) describe a set of dominant values by which they claim the American culture can be explained to people of other countries. This example does not fit neatly into either the general or specific paradigms, being a mixture of both.

The overwhelming practice in orientation programs as described by

Steglitz, Rosenquist Watts, and most authors in this book favors the culture-general approach, although the use of this model may create motivational problems. While most practitioners and scholars prefer culture-general orientation prior to culture-specific, area specialists naturally wish to concentrate on a single culture in depth. Students (as well as faculty and business people) going to a single country appear to favor orientation to only that country. As Nicholson suggested, however, the culture-specific methods used in early Peace Corps orientation may give participants some sense of security, but in the long run it proves inadequate and misleading. Kraemer (1981) voiced even stronger criticism of the culture-specific approach. Experiential learning strategies favor the culture-general perspective as more lasting, relevant, and theoretically sound. Felsing uses it even for groups of students going to the same country. As described by Kuhlman, group orientation for international students in the United States is culture-general because they come from different cultures, despite their common host culture. Koester also calls for a wider use of the culture-general method.

But the issue is not clear cut under many circumstances, such as for teachers of English who face a class composed entirely of students from one country, as Byrd indicates, or for U.S. students who travel widely in several countries on the same trip. Similarly, a practitioner confronted with practical questions such as how to use available resources may well wonder just how useful these seemingly dichotomous theoretical concepts used in culture-general programs really are.

The differences between culture-general and -specific disappear if we learn to think about them in the larger context of international education, with broader educational objectives. When U.S. and foreign students are placed in the same learning environment, including orientation programs, they can create an incredible potential for synergy of learning. We have seen this potential ignite in cross-cultural communication courses composed of equal numbers of U.S. and foreign students. The broadening of objectives effectively sets "superordinate goals" (Brislin 1981; Farnham-Diggory 1972). These not only diffuse possible charges of indoctrination—because U.S. and foreign students are in a position to satisfy each others' learning needs with each others' help—but also render the perceived culture-general/culture-specific dichotomy irrelevant.

This higher level of thinking in "superordinate goals" is essential for those concerned with the newly emerging interest in global perspectives. Increasingly, the international interests of such persons as multinational corporation executives, foreign service personnel of virtually every country, and professionals who manage study abroad and international student offices are truly global. To these people, the dichotomy between culture-general and culture-specific is a false one that needs to be replaced by an emphasis on global thinking. While the topic is beyond the scope of this book, we will return to the "general" and "specific" issue when we deal with sequencing of orientation materials, where the dichotomy emerges persistently.

Cognitive Blindness. Everyone who has decided to travel or study abroad has some knowledge of the host country and makes some assumptions about similarities, differences, and processes of dealing with them. We all carry along a cognitive map, which includes some understanding of our own culture and its relationship with others. On this map the host culture may appear small or large, distorted, incomplete, or far off to one side. Whatever it looks like, the map exists, and it implies certain evaluations, judgments, likes, and dislikes. In addition, individuals make secondary judgments about other cultures: besides what they feel they know already, they have a sense of how much more they wish to know.

Here we run into important ethical and pedagogical problems. If students think they know as much as they wish to know about another culture, they need to be shown the liabilities of this judgment. But it is not enough to show them that they are incorrect or that their knowledge is inadequate, incomplete, or outright false: they need to be persuaded to change. Will our value-free and objective educational tradition tolerate this? Even further, if they fail to realize that they do not know enough—a great many cross-cultural relations are either unknown or exist subconsciously—this knowledge must be brought to their consciousness and made relevant. Many attributions and cognitive distortions occur because people tend to treat what is unknown as being nonexistent; similarly, they understand the complexity of their own culture while failing to see it in other cultures.

This is a good point to leave the discussion of culture and move on to the area of learning about it. In this section, we will return to the question of whether ignorance of other cultures is bliss or a liability for which we pay dearly—even if we fail to realize that we've missed anything. Learning about other cultures is a matter of motivation: How much do we need to know? (or, for many people, What is the minimum we can get by with?)

Learning and Training Concepts

Most trainers, including the authors represented in this book, rely on a single learning theory or concept. This is understandable; otherwise their programs would be very confusing, for there are some eighty learning concepts and theories that deal with such subjects as classification, memory, thinking, reasoning, logic, motivation, attributions, problem-solving, creativity, learning readiness, cognition, ordering, transfer of knowledge,

145

arrival of information, and the like (Mestenhauser 1981, 1983). Many of these concepts are culture-bound and not easily usable; the exceptions include Brislin 1981, 1986; Brislin, Bochner & Lonner 1975; Triandis 1972, 1986; Milton Bennett 1986; Janet Bennett 1986; Christopher 1987; Sikkema and Niyekawa-Howard 1977, 1987; and Hughes-Wiener 1987. New resources are being published regularly by Intercultural Press, Sage Publishers, and Westview Press.

The programs described in this book are heavily dominated by learning approaches that stress competency training for adjustment and survival, and experiential learning strategies. They also refer to specialized skills that assume learning concepts, but these are not clearly identified. For example, Cadman says enrichment programs are needed for A.I.D.-sponsored scholars in order to maximize their effectiveness in transferring technology; enrichment presumes a cognitive process in which one body of knowledge is joined with another. Byrd and Landa speak about augmenting linguistic skills with three additional skills: social, pedagogical, and cross-cultural; this also assumes a confluence of learning. Clarke and Felsing advocate orientation programs with interesting, stimulating, rewarding, and provocative information; these are matters of motivation highly relevant to learning. Clarke also assumes that orientation should provide some training to understand differences, which requires sophisticated intellectual and cultural skills; and as Bennett (1986a) indicates, it requires general cognitive development and an understanding of complexity in which information about opposing cultural characteristics can be retained simultaneously. Baker joins others in describing a three-tiered approach in which three types of training are provided: language, culture, and subject. Nicholson, Soquet, and Mumford Fowler provide the most conceptually sophisticated approaches to learning. Soquet applies Kolb's scheme of different learning styles (Kolb 1979) to the general experiential learning methods used throughout. All these references have implications for orientation content, content sequencing, student motivation, and the nature of adjustment sought. Literature about these concepts is extensive, but is not reflected in the chapters.

International education professionals need not become learning theorists; but if they wish to improve the quality of orientation and enrichment programs, they should be aware of a few key learning issues, especially motivation; some models of learning—experiential, informational, competency, and product learning; adjustment; and sequencing.

Motivation and Culture Learning. Why should students want to attend orientation programs? Or, to avoid the implications of answers to this question, should orientation programs be required? If orientation is as important as we claim, why should it not be required? These questions and others raised in this book relate to motivation, about which we know relatively little, especially cross-culturally. Some of the programs described in this book did not have any problems with it, because orientation was indeed required. However, in most of our universities there is very little agreement about what constitutes international and intercultural knowledge, much less about how it should be imparted, so practitioners are left to their own devices. How can motivation be generated to enhance not only program attendance but the learning that occurs in programs?

Thirty years ago, universities acting *in loco parentis* accepted almost full responsibility for the outcome of the education they provided. Later, at least in this country, students were assumed fully responsible for their learning, while university officials and faculty were considered to be facilitators of such learning. The contemporary tendency is toward a partnership, in which universities have responsibility for motivating as well as teaching students. In this environment, practitioners of international educational exchange programs, who are both educators and processors, have at least half the responsibility to motivate students, sustain their motivation, and teach them self-motivating skills. That responsibility begins with the first contact with the student, often during or just preceding orientation, often in publicity materials.

Ideally, students should be highly motivated to attend orientation programs, which should be stimulating and reinforce the need for learning. They should emerge with knowledge that will help them become effective in the host culture immediately, without "transition" time. More importantly, they should realize that effective functioning in another country requires continuing and conscious effort, which in turn requires a sense of responsibility for their relations with others and self-motivation to sustain them throughout their stay abroad and beyond (despite problems and contingencies that may arise). They should also develop new skills to deal with these contingencies, so they have a sense of confidence.

Wladkowski (1985) suggested that six factors affect motivation: *psychological needs, attitudes, emotions, stimulation, competencies,* and *reinforcements.* All of these factors are culture bound to some extent, which makes motivation a very complex matter. Regarding psychological needs, for example, most of us assume that students going abroad or those coming here for education are highly motivated to succeed (McClelland 1965), and that this motivation is effective throughout their stay. But we also know from experience that students may become so overwhelmed by the host culture (and some of that feeling may even come from orientation programs) that their motivation changes to the need to avoid failure. Similarly, the motivation of students returning home from the United States to their cultures may change to the need for affiliation.

Attitudes that influence motivation may relate to self, teachers, sub-

147

ject matter, or expectations of success or failure. Over-confidence may prevent seeing problems; negative perceptions about a subject (such as statistics, for example) may hinder learning in that subject; an attitude that there is not much to learn from foreigners may isolate a person; an innocent quip about a professor who is perceived as tough or outright prejudiced may create a barrier to learning if a student has to take his or her course; an attitude that nobody cares about foreign students makes it difficult to ask for help when needed; or a perception that people are the same everywhere, good and bad, makes it impossible to acquire cross-cultural insights, no matter how important these may be to transfer of knowledge.

Emotionally, people are likely to work best in fair, friendly, supportive, and achieving environments rather than those in which they are afraid or feel themselves to be manipulated, unfairly outclassed, distrusted, or victims of prejudice and outright discrimination. Today, fear of terrorism and hysteria about unfair competition from abroad affect U.S. students, and arbitrary and tough immigration rules affect foreign students in the United States, tarnishing the environment in which international education should develop. The recent emphasis on competitiveness gives many international students and their sponsors the idea that the United States is exploiting them for commercial reasons. There is an increasing concern in virtually all sending and receiving countries that international students live in self-reinforced "ghettos" and manifest negative attitudes, often toward both their home and host countries. In many instances, host-country nationals do exhibit attitudes of mistrust and outright prejudice toward students from other countries living in their midst. Instead of developing coalitions with those involved in improving the quality of the learning environment, many professionals and students alike seek to depend on support groups, which may help in the short run but in the long run possibly reinforce feelings of self-pity and a siege mentality. Dealing with naive or prejudiced people is a skill, one whose importance will not likely go away in our changing world. Orientation programs should include attention to the establishment of minimum functional trust and confidence in the entire learning environment. They should teach the consequences of intellectual and social isolation, and methods of dealing with fear, anger, feelings of isolation, and dependency.

Stimulation is a measure of attention, interest, and involvement in a subject. The absence or lowest level of stimulation is boredom. Interest studies show that learning experiences should be positive, relaxing, confidence-building, and realistic of accomplishment. They also show something that may come as a surprise to practitioners: required programs need lower levels of stimulation than those attended voluntarily (Wladkowski 1985). Finally, stimulation can increase with the complexity of the tasks introduced. Orientation programs need to be stimulating in order to attract student attendance, and that aspect should be conveyed when the idea of attending is introduced.

Competencies also affect motivation. This can refer to the skills a person brings to a learning situation, but it can also refer to skills a person develops there. When individuals can identify new, useful skills they will learn in a program, their motivation is likely to increase. This is the basis for the competency training learning model described in the next section.

Models of Learning.

Experiential learning. Despite many differences among learning theorists, there is general agreement, even among Soviet psychologists (Talyzina 1981), that all learning is based on experiences. This is the basis of the experiential learning model. When people go abroad, they rely on experiences and skills that they have accumulated in their home countries, many of which can be used in the new setting. This is the assumption made by both Nicholson and Soquet. With additional cross-cultural training, the sojourner will know when prior experience "fits" or does not fit.

But in the rush of American college life, this cross-cultural training is virtually impossible to accomplish either for incoming foreign or outgoing U.S. students. When experiential strategies are employed in the short time available, there is a danger that students assume these "old" experiences will be similar to new ones in the host culture, and the orientation thus only reinforces their ethnocentrism. If ethnocentrism is indeed the natural state for most people (Hanvey 1976), we can easily see how important even minimal training in culture learning is to other types of learning. Unless new learning is integrated with previous learning, the new may be compartmentalized in an individual's mental program and even "double classified" (Farnham-Diggory 1972). This can lead to confusion, anxiety, suppression of the new or the older learned material, or culture shock. Communication theories based on the sender-receiver feedback model may not help detect such double classification, because the individual's feedback can still provide correct answers to questions designed to assess learning. One can see that experiential learning without cross-cultural training is insufficient to permit arrival of new information, even less the grafting of several cognitive skills.

The entire concept of experiential learning may be culture-bound, applicable primarily in cultures of Angle-Saxon background in which learning by doing is a culturally reinforced value. The exclusively experiential orientation programs the author was recently required to set up in Indonesia produced many doubts about effectiveness, transfer of learning value, and appropriateness for Indonesian culture, in which the learning experience is normally didactic and knowledge is commonly "predigested" by others. Similarly, Gamboa's chapter indicated that even northern and

149

southern European students, not to mention Latin American, Asian, and African students, reacted differently to experiential modules.

Information model. Students of social psychology are familiar with the Johari window (Luft 1969), based on mono-cultural interaction, that identifies discrepancies between what people know and do not know about each other. The diagram can be used to explain how Americans can be cognitively blind to some aspects of their own culture that others see clearly, and vice versa. In addition, it shows how some areas of knowledge can be unknown to both parties and thus open to mutual and reciprocal discovery. Practitioners of orientation programs may find this a useful tool in orientation. (Without such tools and concepts, it is extremely hard to tell people that they do not understand themselves!)

Most of us, including the authors of our chapters, still assume that people come to new situations with a *tabula rasa.* The information model of orientation assumes that if people can learn enough information, they

JOHARI WINDOW*

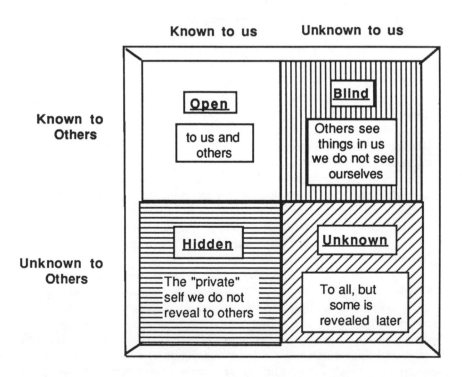

* Based on Luft (1969)

will know how to behave. This is often the case; there are areas of "cognitive blindness" that can be filled. Simply providing data has been an excellent way out of the ethical dilemma, allowing orientation practitioners to maintain a neutral, objective learning posture. But experience shows that the information model is very unreliable. Information is forgotten, misplaced in memory, used as "evidence" in unintended or inaccurate ways, or cognitively isolated and thus irrelevant to understanding a culture because it does not fit into a needed conceptual frame of reference.

Practitioners are familiar with examples of discovery learning, the "lightbulb" that flashes when an individual suddenly discovers meaning for a previously meaningless, "loose" piece of information. Orientation programs often produce such delayed reactions: information collected during orientation suddenly comes to life when the individual encounters practical situations or problems in which it is useful. Experimental evidence suggests, however, that even if they know the cross-cultural issues involved, individuals can subconsciously tune out a foreign speaker whose accent they dislike or whose nationality is out of favor (Nisbett & Wilson 1977). Some research being developed suggests that foreign teaching assistants are subject to this phenomenon (Brown 1987).

Another variation of cognitive blindness that should be of interest to orientation practitioners is what learning psychologists call "unconscious use of information" (Farnham-Diggory 1972). This occurs when a previously known set of data is fixed into association with other meanings and requires "unfixing" through "priming," or recall. Because the original fixing probably originated in the home country, host-country orientation may provide the first "unfixing." This did not emerge in the chapters, but a dramatic example occurred in Indonesia recently. A scholar preparing for graduate studies in the United States attended an orientation program where information was provided in a didactic fashion about the American analytical tradition, which requires a sense of independence, ability to question sources, and self-propelled motivation to search and discover answers. Translated into his own cognitive and cultural language, the message came through as, "When you are in the United States, you will not get help from anybody and will be all on your own." A few months later, program administrators discovered him living in the United States with a "siege mentality," associating only with other Indonesians.

The best-known method of dealing with this fixed knowledge problem is to emphasize learning-how-to-learn (Triandis 1986). Soquet and Nicholson subscribe to this idea in their chapters, but appear to believe that learning-how-to-learn happens simply by learning from experiences in a traditional experiential mode. But the ability to learn-how-to-learn cross-culturally requires a more complex conceptual framework, enabling the individual to find a higher-level category of cognition similar to the

151

"superordinate goal" mentioned in the last section. Individuals, American or foreign, who understand this process will gain enormously from such cognitive insights. They will ease the stress on their memories, learn to "unfix" information stuck in inappropriate bins, connect previously unrelated pieces, gain self-confidence, decrease their sense of dependency stemming from uncertainty about ignorance, enhance their creativity, improve their ability to transfer knowledge to practical problems, and renew their knowledge after leaving the educational institution.

Now let us look at the information-based orientation programs from the point of view of arrival-of-information theories, the concepts by which computers are designed. Most orientation educators are under great pressure to pack a vast amount of information into predeparture or on-arrival programs, all very necessary and useful but difficult to digest cognitively for many good reasons. Most practitioners respond to this problem by reducing information to handouts and handbooks, creating peer advising support systems, organizing host family stays, or creating a bond of trust with the students so they will come for help when they need it. Concepts and theories are probably the last things we would consider including in an orientation program, on the grounds that these students need practical information, not theories. But if we examine arrival-of-information theories, we find that information overload is caused not by the quantity of information, but by the absence of an appropriate conceptual framework in the minds of the departing or arriving students.

How does the information model work? New information is most commonly processed through short-term memory before it reaches long-term memory, where it can be retained and ready for recall. New information is processed in short-term memory only if it is already familiar to one's "program," e.g., if there is a cognitive category for it, if there is no awareness of major cultural difference that may provoke an emotional reaction against it, and if there is no other barrier such as negative attributions (Triandis 1986; Brislin 1981, 1986). An individual highly trained in rote memory, as many foreign students are, may be able to retain a great deal of information even without pre-existing categories, but then must usually establish new categories for them. A large number of such free-standing categories increases overload and fatigue. Furthermore, the information will not be readily recalled in connection with another category. In several clinical experiences, we worked with international students who failed their qualifying examinations for graduate degrees because they were asked the "wrong" questions. When straight-recall questions were asked, they could recite the information requested. Experts say that once such information gets into the wrong "bin," it can be difficult to transfer it to the right one even if the person is aware of the error. This has many practical implications for orientation, which will be described in Chapter 18.

An individual can absorb a great deal of new information if it is presented with a conceptual framework. Then complexity is not to be feared and avoided, but encouraged, if introduced as part of training in cultural relativism with added emphasis on complexity (Triandis 1986). In other words, the more variables that are known, the more explanations there are to choose from, thus reducing the chances for negative attributions. This point runs counter to assumptions shared by most of our authors—that orientation must be simple, uncomplicated, and careful of possible information overload. Greater complexity can enhance stimulation and thus motivation, as noted earlier. The issue instead is not how much information is provided, but how it is presented, timed, and integrated.

Competency Training. Competency-based training is an alternative to the didactic information model and the experiential model. It bypasses some of the controversies involved in them, including the issue of culture-general versus culture-specific. The ultimate goal of cross-cultural orientation should be to facilitate not only peoples' survival in other cultures, as important as that may be, but also their functioning in the performance of tasks for which they are abroad (such as studying, teaching, doing research, conducting business, negotiating, or consulting). These tasks require certain competencies. Training in such competencies is consistent with contemporary trends in higher education, which emphasize outcomes rather than "seat time" spent in an educational institution. In this volume, only the EIL and the Peace Corps described their programs as competency-based, although others included training in several personal competencies, such as flexibility, adjustability, and openness.

Before undertaking a serious training program, including initial orientation to "nuts and bolts," we need to know the nature of the tasks that individuals are expected to perform in the foreign cultures. In this book, only the Peace Corps has conducted a thorough analysis of every job the volunteers will perform. In educational exchanges, the only research we have was conducted on classroom-related differences between the United States and two other cultures (by Hoff [1979]). More research needs to be done on the analysis of educational functions in different cultures and different clusters of fields, because the competencies and intellectual skills that need to be developed can vary by culture and discipline.

Such research may be at the very heart of the debate on the internationalization of disciplines. It is likely, for example, that students from technical and scientific fields do not see the relevance of some of the concepts defined earlier, and therefore do not respond well to cross-cultural orientation programs except those immediately practical to them (such as logistics and nuts-and-bolts). They may feel that the intellectual competencies used in their disciplines do not vary across cultures and that cross-cultural programs should be given to students in disciplines in which they do. It is our premise that all students need cross-cultural training, because culture is a variable, if not in the actual study of their discipline, then certainly in knowing how the knowledge of their discipline is used, how professionals are regarded by others, how scientific tasks are implemented, how they secure cooperation with others, how they organize their work, what ethical considerations they must observe, how they renew knowledge, and in general how they function within their culture as professionals. Hofstede (1984) has documented this point exceptionally well in connection with business administration and management in more than fifty countries, and Hawes and Kealey (1979) persuaded others about the dominant significance of cross-cultural competencies for technicians working in foreign aid projects.

Most cross-cultural scholars focus on interpersonal competencies—communication skills, or such personality attributes as adjustability, flexibility, and openness. The best and most relevant treatment of these can be found in Paige (1986). Unfortunately, practitioners concentrate on these competencies to the virtual exclusion of other equally, if not more important, cognitive competencies.

The one "hub" intellectual competency is comparative thinking. Comparative thinking presumes the ability to think critically and analytically and to master problem solving. There are literally dozens of resources on our campuses for the development of these skills. They need to be augmented with the cultural insights to permit cross-cultural comparisons. Every student involved in a cross-cultural situation compares things regularly and makes assumptions about similarities, differences, relevancies, and relationships (real or perceived) whether trained in comparative analysis or not. Orientation programs should be, and often are, designed to train students to be aware of differences. Teaching comparative skills in turn requires several other skills: differentiation, attribution, and emic and etic thinking. Together, these contribute to understanding complexity and are a necessary prerequisite to another intellectual skill in great demand—creativity. Contact of cultures has been historically the most common method of creativity training; this fact is so obvious to professionals that it is difficult to understand why the public does not recognize it or support the programs that produce such a valuable commodity.

Developing these skills takes a great deal of time. Although many orientation programs, including some of those described here, do include content about study skills, and such study skills are also commonly taught as part of language training, they are usually too limited to accomplish broader objectives. But with all the resources available on our campuses, and with the cooperative and networking skills we do possess, it should be possible to call on others to help develop meaningful approaches to cognitive competence-training programs. Comparative thinking can be taught in cooperation with cross-culturally educated study-skill professionals and faculty members. Methods of instruction, including carefully selected experiential modules, are available.

Orientation Content: Product or Process? The distinction that some learning psychologists make between "product" and "process" learning is not clear cut, but is useful for making a few generalizations about the ideal content of orientation programs. "Product" learning, to which most academic disciplines are oriented, is an organized body of learning represented by a quantum of knowledge, which a person can be shown to have. "Process" learning is the study of how to think or learn. Obviously, most disciplines also include "process" learning. Other disciplines do focus on process. The distinction is demonstrated in the contemporary controversy surrounding colleges of education. "Content" courses represent the "product"-oriented disciplines, such as the sciences and social sciences; they tell *what* to teach. The so-called "methods" courses represent the education courses that tell how to teach. The greatest difficulty in determining the content of orientation programs is often a similar confusion between "product" and "process" learning concepts (Farnham-Diggory 1972).

Let us first look at the great variety of ways in which the authors represented in the chapters identified the content of their orientation programs. First, the content was not differentiated between American and foreign clientele, and thus was "generic." Secondly, shorter and one-shot programs appear to concentrate commonly on "nuts and bolts" and "survival" orientation (Baker and Kuhlman). This choice is consistent with the counseling and human-relations development concepts, which suggest that individuals must first deal with their immediate, "up front" needs. International students get a heavy dose of information about immigration regulations, which represent a unique content specific to their stay here. Similarly, orientation for U.S. students is increasingly concerned with safety, emergencies, legal systems abroad, and processing skills, such as transportation, lodging, and costs.

Not surprisingly, the rest of the content comes from inter-disciplinary approaches to cross-cultural relations and cross-cultural communication: American culture and civilization, international relations or specific-country relations with the United States, and comparative education. These appear to be used for both international and U.S. students, as Cadman, Sarles, Felsing, Clarke, and O'Driscoll demonstrate. Where language preparation is necessary, as indicated by Byrd, O'Driscoll, and Baker, language will naturally be a large part of the content. Koester feels, however, that language skill-training is neglected in typical orientations, and she urges that new approaches be developed on the grounds that 22 percent of U.S. students desire to improve their language skills. These students are majors in fields other than foreign languages who seek to augment their education through study abroad.

With a few exceptions, we are struck by the lack of systematic thought given to subject selection for orientation, to integration of subjects when they come from different disciplines, and to the intellectual skills these disciplines contribute. Part of the difficulty is undoubtedly in the clientele, who do not appear to know clearly what kind of preparation they need among the vast possibilities (as Steglitz suggests). Another difficulty stems from the need to present a lot of material in a greatly condensed and abstracted form, which may either be too simple or too general to relate to the sojourners' needs. A third difficulty, suggested by Martin and Hammer (1987), is that students have greater confidence in their abilities to manage abroad before they depart than after they return, by which time they know best what they should have had and what they missed.

But as we have suggested, the greatest difficulty is the problem between the "product" and "process" learning. Practitioners would have an impossible task if they were to include all the knowledge with some bearing on the prospective trip abroad: history, geography, languages, government, politics, social structure, economics, trade, foreign relations, popular culture, arts, music, literature ... in short, virtually everything, because everything has some importance in understanding any culture. If a student then visits more than one country, the same amount of content might have to be included for each. International education professionals appear to have instead designed—individually and institutionally—a "core content" for a generic introduction to study abroad for all students, which they can squeeze into the time available for those interested enough to attend. Most of this knowledge is process oriented, directed toward how to survive and function in other cultures. Offering any other content would require difficult choices, such as evaluations of what discipline is more important and which faculty members must be invited to make presentations. If such choices are made, the preference usually is for faculty who support interdisciplinary studies, liberal arts subjects, or comparatively-based disciplines.

No matter what content is chosen, orientation conveys important messages. A likely message is that orientation must not be very important if it can be squeezed into a very short time. This, combined with the psychological proximity to the rest of the world due to television and travel, can lead students to believe that they already know more than such a brief introduction can offer. Another message to faculty is that orientation programs are too "soft" to be of interest to them. Finally, process-oriented core concepts are out of synchronization with the mainstream of academic life, which continues to emphasize heavily the specialized, disciplinary, product-learning approach.

Consider how very important these questions are in our universities. They dominate the classroom, research laboratories, and examination systems, as well as the thinking of exchange sponsors, parents, employers, consumers, and university sponsors. Consider, too, various contemporary trends, such as the debate about inflation of education, the calls to excellence and quality, and the need to return to the basics (Adler 1982; Astin 1985; Boyer 1983, 1987; College Board 1983; National Commission on Excellence 1982; Smart 1985; Task Force on Federal Elementary and Secondary Education Policy 1983; Trow 1974). Consider further the persistent suggestions about teaching more subjects and content (not process, method, and survival) to maintain international competitiveness (Atlantic Council 1987; Egon Zender 1986; Global Perspectives in Education 1987), the recent effort to establish a minimum knowledge Americans should have about themselves (Hirsch 1987; Bloom 1987; Degler 1977), and studies undertaken to establish what students in this country know about the world (Barrows 1981; Michigan State University 1984; Woyzach 1987). These works, largely unknown to international educators, demonstrate the emphasis on product learning that comes primarily from traditional disciplines.

We must acknowledge that product learning appears to be the contemporary trend in higher education. And really, what good is it to know how to communicate with one another if we do not know what to communicate about? Orientation programs must include some specialized approaches from the disciplines if we wish to be relevant to the academic missions of our universities.

We should recognize that preparation for study abroad is not accomplished only in the orientation programs that we sponsor: students already come with academic background and preparation that we should take into account. In addition, they have a certain amount of motivation to learn by themselves, which scholars of adult learning have described well. We should discuss with our academic colleagues from the various disciplines what their fields can offer to a variety of students with different focuses on international learning. Serious students of area studies, including American studies, will have different learning needs from those who go abroad for the first time briefly on a "reconnaissance" sojourn.

Hanvey (1976) identified "cross-cultural sophistications," such as cross-cultural effectiveness, scholarship, openness, and transculturality. Depending on the goals of the students and their initial level of sophistication, orientation programs may need to vary the mix of product and process learning. Students should plan on achieving either on their own or through regular classroom sessions. In fact, our discussions with teaching faculty might prove very interesting and productive in additional ways: they may face the same questions and problems with product and process learning themselves. For example, what is the "core" amount of knowledge a student in engineering should have before going to the Soviet Union? Out of the literally thousands of books on the Soviet Union, are one or two especially suitable for general background and preparation? What about foreign students coming to the United States? If there are no such books, how should we teach the students to learn-how-to-learn the missing parts for themselves through contacts with the people of their host countries?

Orientation and Adjustment. According to Baker, the bulk of orientation content at his university pertains to "survival." Rosenquist Watts reported that 73 percent of the respondents to her survey listed "survival" as the dominant content for U.S. students. Virtually every chapter in this book makes a reference to survival, adjustment (Felsing), coping skills (Steglitz), personal safety (Nicholson), readiness for academic work (Cadman), dealing with stress (Byrd), adaptation to change (Mumford Fowler), overcoming insecurities, uneasiness, or apprehension (Koester), or dealing with unrealistic expectations as a method of preventing or lessening culture shock (Clarke). Byrd commented that even language teachers may occasionally suffer from culture shock.

Since so much effort is being spent on adjustment but so little stated about it explicitly, we treat it here as a separate issue of orientation. It still is a learning issue, however, because most of the effort is being directed to knowledge about cross-cultural adjustment, and about sources and causes of maladjustment. This overwhelming concern with problems of adjustment, which appears to be more commonly stressed in orientation for U.S. participants, needs to be explained conceptually, because it demonstrates cross-cultural learning problems.

The conceptualization stems primarily from our democratic values, which stress happiness and actuation; from human relations education, which advocates the maximum development of the individual's potential; and from theories of work and employment. Americans are also psychology-wiser than people elsewhere. In this context, adjustment concerns have meaning and are readily accepted. But telling foreign students to attend orientation programs in order to achieve a healthier adjustment may make no sense to them, and even cause problems: it requires a cross-cultural literacy beyond individual survival skills. First, "adjusting" implies overcoming problems, and having problems is a negatively loaded concept in most cultures. Brislin (1981) suggests that negative concepts require culturally sensitive, perhaps culture-specific, explanations. Similarly, rules and regulations tend to have a negative loading, making a simple, factual presentation of the rules and consequences of violation grossly inadequate. Second, adjustment implies a certain degree of conformity to another culture, which may imply a loss of one's identity.

Third, if adjustment's goal is general satisfaction with the stay, what does satisfaction mean? Many cultures do not have a concept of general satisfaction equivalent to ours. People think of different kinds of satisfaction relating to such things as learning, academic progress, personal affairs, relationships with members of the opposite sex, professional accomplishments, intellectual environment, and financial affairs. If there is a general satisfaction, it probably occurs when specific satisfactions accumulate; however, a lack of satisfaction in a particularly dominant area may influence other areas.

Fourth, the cause of poor satisfaction is difficult to assess. Our tendency is to assume that dissatisfaction is due to the nature of an experience: if only things would change, then satisfaction would follow. Unfortunately, certain experiences—such as dealing with rules, regulations, and academic requirements—are inevitable, which suggests that an individual may have to change to achieve satisfaction. But human change also carries negative loading in many cultures. Obviously, social change is an implicit component of international education. Although detailed discussion of social change is beyond the scope of this chapter, it should be borne in mind that change affects individuals differently and at different times—and not always negatively. Furthermore, it is not always a matter of personal adjustment, a personality variable; time orientation is one of the universal cultural-value orientations (Kluckhohn & Strodtbeck 1961) that can determine people's behavior (Hofstede 1984).

Theories of work, from which the adjustment concepts also derive, define adjustment as a form of relationship (correspondence) between individuals and their environment (Culha 1974). The nature of such correspondence varies depending on the values the individuals may seek in the relationship (e.g., harmony, balance, reciprocity, control, complement, suitability, and agreement). Each of these possible relationships represents values (here comes culture again!) and behavior. Depending on these, then, adjustment may be the responsibility of the individual, as in our culture, or of natural forces (fate).

These are not the meanings of adjustment that practitioners have in mind. Most of us think of it in functional terms and expect that students will accomplish such adjustment in a relatively short period of time. Our university systems are tolerant, and often grant exceptions and special considerations to achieve the adjustment. This attitude demonstrates the social psychological relationship of majority and minority: if students fail to adjust in a reasonably short time, or if they continue to seek exceptions, their credibility—and often the credibility of our offices—will be jeopardized.

To complicate things even further, many societies and cultures make basic assumptions about "ideally adjusted" personality types. For example, our cultural ideal of a "democratic personality" involves tolerance and achievement. By comparison, the Soviet Union has a very well defined concept of a "socialist personality" (*Practice, Problems, and Prospects of Socialism*, 1979). Cultural anthropologists are familiar with similar personality types, such as the Japanese, Filipino, or Asian personality (Doi 1973; Bulatao 1964; Lebra 1976; Lynch 1964). Many religious groups, such as the Muslims, also assume a certain ideal personality type. The current Turkish government is said to be introducing a concept of the ideal Turkish personality (religious, obedient, submissive, and cooperative). Foreign students in the United States and other democratic countries have a special problem with "adjustment" because our societies permit a range of behaviors often bordering on extremes, with reinforcement available. They may become easily confused and disoriented, experience stress, and need assistance. Our services for foreign students, which we are often hard pressed to explain or justify, can be considered a price we pay for a free society. The services and their dedicated personnel are specially trained to provide an infrastructure for those in stress (Burak 1987).

Finally, there are major cross-cultural and pedagogical issues involved in the way we present adjustment to our audiences. At the time of orientation, the problems that are supposed to cause maladjustment have not occurred yet. We have developed elaborate strategies to anticipate them—participatory, didactic, and experiential. They include the *Bafá Bafá* simulation game, case studies, use of veteran foreign and U.S. students, descriptions of available services, and discussion of the culture-shock U-curve. This book provides many examples of such educational methodologies, but the choice of methods is actually not very large, seeming to involve a preference for experiential or didactic strategy (or their combination). Steglitz found that respondents to her survey of foreign student orientation programs use the experiential model less frequently than do programs for U.S. student orientation, especially programs at the EIL and in the Peace Corps, where it is used exclusively. The lesser use of experiential strategies for foreign students may relate to language difficulties, but possibly such strategies are culture-specific and thus inapplicable for multicultural audiences. Although Gamboa claimed that these methods could be used, his data suggested significant variations in responses among various cultural groupings. Furthermore, his research did not address the transfer of experiences intended by the trainers, for which more conclusive research is needed. Many trainers utilizing experiential methods strain to establish the impression that transfer of knowledge is occurring, even when they are doing little more than putting words into the mouths of intended targets audiences. To establish cross-cultural equivalencies of experiences requires a high degree of skill in comparative analysis, as was discussed in the competency model of learning above.

Sequencing of Materials. Not enough attention is paid to the way in which topics and materials are sequenced in orientation programs. Organizers are greatly limited by time, pressure to include certain topics (e.g., immigration rules), availability of resource persons, shortage of funds, and random suggestions from various planning committees.

The lack of conscious attention to sequencing in even sophisticated programs may not be due only to fiscal and time constraints. Practitioners may suspect that cross-cultural learners have their own natural cognitive skills for ordering new experiences. This is consistent with some research: Simon (1967) suggested that most people do in fact have an "internal organizer" that helps them arrange and supervise attention they will give to different activities. His theory maintains that there are basically two ways to do this. The first is through lining one activity after another, usually spread out over time, a common way in which individuals solve potential conflicts of attention. The second way is by selecting a higher-level goal composed of several sub-goals, not unlike the "superordinate goal" used in conflict resolution. This permits an individual to incorporate several sub-goals at once, simultaneously placing them into a broader perspective. The second method is less commonly used, but preferable. It allows students and professionals to put the issue of "time" (which is itself the higher-level concept of sequencing) into a cross-cultural perspective so they do not need to consider their own or the host culture as interfering with their internal organizers. This idea is not evident in the orientation programs we have examined, however.

Yet practitioners do make sequencing decisions, even if unconsciously, and they make assumptions about how the program materials "hang together." What are some of these assumptions? That various topics are unrelated, and thus the sequence does not matter? That everything is new and elementary to sojourners, so orientation is just introductory material to the actual stay abroad, which is the more advanced sequel? Only Soquet made explicit assumptions about the order of topical presentations, but others made more implicit assumptions. Whenever authors refer to language training, they assume sequencing materials linearly from basic to intermediate to advanced. Kuhlman's chapter orders content chronologically, from prearrival to class attendance. The Peace Corps program is serial, with one experience following another. The EIL program appears to be sequenced hierarchically, with the most basic concepts forming the foundation for others, which are added on top like building blocks. Such sequencing follows Maslowian theories of the hierarchy of human needs. Developmental psychological approaches also use the building-block concepts, but combine them with serial sequencing, one stage following another (Bennett 1986b).

When orientation programs include content about the home culture in relation to the host-country culture, the sequential ordering may be either reductionist or expansive, depending on whether we assume that home culture knowledge is a condition for knowing others. In any case, knowledge of one must come first. Examples of both sequences are implicit in Sarles. One might be inclined to agree with Hanvey (1976), Bennett (1986a), and Alger (1983) that people are socialized in a progression from individual to family to village community to state or province to region to nation and finally to the world—with the understanding that the final step from national to international requires a significant cognitive shift. But if this kind of sequencing of materials is used with students, it becomes in fact neither reductionist nor expansive but hierarchical, which has extremely important psychological and ethical consequences. Moving from local to state to national to international can imply gaining higher levels of knowledge and perspective with each step, with the first levels declining in importance. Most students, American and foreign, are not prepared to accept such a hierarchy.

This has practical implications in and beyond orientation. Whether we choose the "briefing" or the "education" plan, orientation may be the first time a student is introduced to this apparent dichotomy between home and other cultures. Until another culture is introduced, the socialization sequence from one's own person and family to the international community is only theoretical and logical; but in an encounter with another culture one is touched personally, and the resulting learning could be different both quantitatively and qualitatively (Sikkema & Niyekawa-Howard 1977, 1987). If one has to that point denied differences or seen the rest of the world as an extension of his or her own culture, symptoms of cognitive revolution appear. It matters little which comes first, knowledge of the home culture or a foreign culture: in the actual cross-cultural encounter, they come simultaneously and feed each other. This recognition has led some scholars to search for a different way of perceiving the apparent dichotomy between national and international sequences. They have developed concepts that transcend them both theoretically and practically. The two most prominent of these concepts are the "third culture" (Useem & Donaghue 1963) and the "multicultural man" (Dinges 1983; Adler 1977).

We are now back at our starting point: one cannot talk about orientation without conceptualizing the entire educational experience abroad and its expected outcome. Or, stated differently, it is impossible to study a subject without understanding its cultural context. The sequencing problem forces us to deal with this fact. To do so, we must use concepts about outcomes that take the sojourner's degree of cross-cultural sophistication into account. There is a great deal of work ahead to develop such concepts and integrate them into orientation programs.

References

Adler, N.J. 1982. *The Paideia proposal: An educational manifesto.* New York: Macmillan.

Adler, Peter. 1977. Beyond cultural identity: Reflections upon cultural and multicultural man. In Richard Brislin, ed., *Cultural learning: Concepts, applications and research.* Honolulu, Hawaii: University of Hawaii.

Alger, Chadwick F. April 1983. Human development: A micro and macro perspective. Paper presented at the 24th annual convention of the International Studies Association, Mexico City.

Amir, Y. 1969. Contact hypothesis in ethnic relations. *Psychological Bulletin* 71:319–342.

Astin, Alexander. 1985. *Achieving educational excellence.* San Francisco: Jossey-Bass.

The Atlantic Council of the United States and the Citizens Network for Foreign Affairs. 1987. U.S. international leadership for the 21st century: Building a national foreign affairs constituency. Report of the Joint Working Group of The Atlantic Council of the United States and the Citizens Network for Foreign Affairs. Washington, D.C.: The Atlantic Council of the United States.

Barrows, Thomas et al. 1981. College students' knowledge and beliefs: A survey of global understanding. The final report of the Global Understanding Project. Educational Testing Service, New Rochelle, NY: Change Magazine Press.

Bennett, Janet M. 1986. Modes of cross-cultural training: Conceptualizing cross-cultural training as education. *International Journal of Intercultural Relations* (10)2.

Bennett, Milton J. 1986a. A developmental approach to training for intercultural sensitivity: New applications for cross-cultural orientation. *International Journal of Intercultural Relations* 10(2).

_____. 1986b. Towards ethnorelativism: A development model of intercultural sensitivity. In R. Michael Paige, ed., *Cross-cultural orientation: New conceptualizations and applications.* Lanham, MD: University Press of America.

Bloom, Alan. 1987. *The closing of the American mind.* New York: Simon and Schuster.

Boyer, Ernest L. 1987. *College, the undergraduate experience in America.* New York: Harper & Row.

_____. 1983. *High school: A report on secondary education in America.* The

Carnegie Foundation for the Advancement of Teaching. New York: Harper & Row.

Brislin, Richard W. 1986. A culture general assimilator: Preparation for various types of sojourns. *International Journal of Intercultural Relations* 10(2).

_____. 1981. *Cross-cultural encounters: Face-to-face interaction.* New York: Pergamon.

Brislin, Richard W. and Paul Pedersen. 1976. *Cross-cultural orientation programs.* New York: Gardner Press, Inc.

Brislin, Richard W., S. Bochner, and W. J. Lonner, eds. 1975. *Cross-cultural perspectives on learning.* New York: John Wiley & Sons.

Broome, Benjamin J. 1978. A culture-specific framework for teaching intercultural communication. Paper presented at the annual conference of the International Communication Association, Dallas.

Brown, Kimberly. May 1987. Effects of perceived country of origin, educational status, and ascribed native speakerness on American college student attitude toward non-native instructors. Ph.D. dissertation. University of Minnesota, Minneapolis, MN.

Bulatao, Jaime, S. J. 1964. The manileno's mainsprings. *Four readings on Philippine values.* Quezon City: Ateneo de Manila University Press.

Burak, Patricia A. 1987. *Crisis management in a cross-cultural setting.* Washington, D.C.: NAFSA.

Christopher, Elizabeth. 1987. Academia: A cross-cultural problem. *International Journal of Intercultural Relations* 11(2):191-206.

The College Board. 1983. *Academic preparation for college: What students need to know and be able to do.* New York: College Board.

Culha, Meral. 1974. Needs and satisfaction of foreign students at the University of Minnesota. Ph.D. dissertation, University of Minnesota, Minneapolis, MN.

Degler, Carl N. 1977. *Out of our past,* revised. Scranton, PA: Harper & Row.

Dinges, Norman. 1983. Intercultural competence. In Dan Landis and Richard Brislin, eds., *Handbook of intercultural training volume I.* New York: Pergamon.

Doi, Takeo. 1973. *The anatomy of dependence.* New York, NY: Kodanska International, Ltd. (through Harper & Row).

Donald, Janet G. 1985. Intellectual skills in higher education. *The Canadian Journal of Higher Education,* 15(1):53–68.

Egon Zender International. 1986. Global competition: Are U.S. companies meeting the challenge? *Corporate Issues Monitor* 1(3).

Farnham-Diggory, S. 1972. *Cognitive process in education.* New York: Harper & Row.

Global Perspectives in Education. 1987. The United States prepares for its future: Global perspectives in education. Report of the Study Commission on Global Education. New York: Global Perspectives in Education, Inc.

Hanvey, Robert G. 1976. *An attainable global perspective: Center for war and peace studies.* New York: Global Perspectives in Education, Inc.

Hirsch, E. D. 1987. *Cultural literacy: What every American needs to know.* Boston: Houghton Mifflin Co.

Hoff, Bernardine L. R. 1979. Classroom-generated barriers to learning: International students in American higher education. Ph.D. Dissertation, U.S. International University, San Diego, CA.

Hofstede, Geert. 1984. *Culture's consequences: International differences in work-related values.* Beverly Hills, CA: Sage Publications.

Howell, William S. 1977. Can intercultural communication be taught in a classroom? In David Hoopes ed., *Readings in intercultural communication volume III.* Pittsburgh: The Society for Intercultural Education, Training and Research.

Kluckhohn, Florence & Fred L. Strodtbeck. 1961. *Variations in value orientations.* Westport, CT: Greenwood Press.

Knowles, M. S. 1980. *The modern practice of adult education: From pedagogy to andragogy.* Chicago: Follett.

Koester, Jolene. 1987. *A profile of the U.S. student abroad—1984 and 1985.* New York: Council on International Educational Exchange.

Kohls, L. Robert. 1988. Models for comparing and contrasting cultures. In Joy Reid, ed., *Building professional dimensions of educational exchange.* Yarmouth, ME: Intercultural Press, Inc.

Kolb, David. 1979. *Organizational psychology: An experiential approach.* Englewood Cliffs, NJ: Prentice Hall, Inc.

Kraemer, Alfred J. August 1981. The intercultural experience as a planned learning experience. Paper presented at the annual convention of the American Psychological Association, Los Angeles.

Lebra, Takie Sugiyama. 1976. *Japanese patterns of behavior.* Honolulu: University of Hawaii Press.

Luft, Joseph. 1969. *Of human interaction.* Palo Alto, CA: National Press Books.

Lynch, Frank, S. J. 1964. Social acceptance. *Four readings on Philippine values.* Quezon City: Ateneo de Manila University Press.

McClelland, David. 1961. *The achieving society.* Princeton, NJ: Van Nostrand, Publishers.

Martin, Judith N. and Mitchell R. Hammer. 1987. Behavior categories of intercultural communication competence: Everyday communicators' perceptions. Paper presented at the Annual Conference of the Society for Intercultural Education, Training and Research in Toronto, Canada, May 1987.

Maslow, Abraham H. 1954. *Motivation and personality.* New York: Harper and Row.

Mestenhauser, Josef A. 1983. Learning from sojourners. In Dan Landis and Richard Brislin, eds., *Handbook of intercultural relations volume II.* New York: Pergamon.

_____. 1981. Selected learning concepts and theories. In Gary Althen, ed., *Learning across cultures.* Washington, D.C.: NAFSA.

165

Michigan State University. 1984. *Critical needs for international education at Michigan State University in the mid-1980s.* East Lansing, MI: International Studies and Programs, Michigan State University.

Moscovici, Serge. 1976. Social influence and social change. London: Academic Press.

National Academy of Engineering. 1987. *Strengthening U.S. engineering through international cooperation.* Washington, D.C.: National Academy of Engineering.

National Commission on Excellence in Education. April 1983. *A nation at risk.* Washington, D.C.

National Commission on Higher Education Issues. November 1982. To strengthen quality in higher education: Summary recommendations of the national commission on higher education issues. Washington, D.C.: American Council on Education.

Nisbett, Richard E. and Timothy DeCamp Wilson. 1977. The halo effect: Evidence of unconscious alteration of judgment. *Journal of Personality and Social Psychology* 35(4):250–256.

Paige, R. Michael, ed. 1986. *Cross-cultural orientation: New conceptualizations and applications.* Lanham, MD: University Press of America.

Practice, problems and prospects of socialism. 1979. Moscow, U.S.S.R.: Progress Publishers.

Saltzman, Carol E. 1986. One hundred and fifty percent persons: Guides to orienting international students. In R. Michael Paige, ed., *Cross-cultural orientation: New conceptualizations and applications.* Lanham, MD: University Press of America.

Sikkema, Mildred and Agnes M. Niyekawa-Howard. 1977. *Cross-cultural learning and self-growth.* New York: International Association of Schools of Social Work.

_____. 1987. *Design for cross-cultural learning.* Yarmouth, ME: Intercultural Press.

Simon, Herbert A. 1967. Motivation and emotional control of cognition. *Psychological Review* 74:29–39.

Smart, John C., ed. 1985. *Higher education: Handbook of theory and research volume 1.* New York: Agathon Press.

Stewart, Edward D. 1972. *American culture patterns: A cross-cultural perspective.* La Grange Park, IL: Intercultural Network.

Talyzina, Nina. 1981. *The psychology of learning.* Moscow: Progress Publications.

Task Force on Federal Elementary and Secondary Education Policy. 1983. *Making the grade.* New York: Twentieth Century Fund.

Triandis, Harry C. 1986. Approaches to cross-cultural orientation and the role of culture assimilator training. In R. Michael Paige, ed., *Cross-cultural orientation: New conceptualizations and applications.* Lanham, MD: University Press of America.

_____. 1972. *The analysis of subjective culture.* New York: Wiley-Interscience.

Trow, Martin. 1974. Higher education and moral development. Proceedings of the 1984 Educational Testing Service Invitational Conference—Moral Development.

Princeton, NJ: Educational Testing Service.

Useem, John R. and J. Donoghue. 1963. Men in the middle of the third culture. *Human Organization* 22(3).

Vogel, Ezra. 1979. *Japan as number one.* New York: Harper.

Westwood, M.J., Scott Lawrence, and Rorri McBlane. 1986. New dimensions in orientation of international students. In R. Michael Paige, ed., *Cross-cultural orientation: New conceptualizations and applications.* Lanham, MD: University Press of America.

Wladkowski, Raymond J. 1985. *Enhancing adult motivation to learn.* San Francisco: Jossey-Bass.

Woyzach, Robert B. 1987. Understanding the global arena. *Quarterly Report* 11(4). Columbus, OH: Ohio State University, The Mershon Center.

18

Adding the Disciplines: From Theory to Relevant Practice

Josef A. Mestenhauser

The Missing Ingredient: The Academic Disciplines

The role of students' academic disciplines in cross-cultural orientation has been conspicuously absent in the preceding chapters. Is cross-cultural orientation, then, academically irrelevant to most other fields of study, unless for students at American liberal arts colleges whose purpose for study abroad is to enhance their liberal education? Otherwise, the only academically relevant orientation appears to be a program for foreign students coming to the United States, offered at the Economics Institute of the University of Colorado, where those attending are oriented to the way economics is taught in the United States.

If a person is well adjusted and settled in the foreign culture, the thinking goes, academic progress will surely follow. The relationship between academic study and orientation, therefore, is often an assumed division of labor between international education professionals, who take care of the cross-cultural orientation, and faculty, who are in charge of the academics. This division of labor is reinforced by a common organizational pattern in universities that places study abroad and foreign student advising in the area of student affairs rather than academic affairs. In addition to the structural separation, there is a strongly held perception that narrowly-defined educational goals supercede all others, as if individuals can divide their lives into two distinct parts. Adjustment-dominated orientation rationales accept this division. Their underlying human-relations concepts hold that in the hierarchy of human needs, the more basic needs (such as adjustment) must be satisfied before "higher" academic needs. Yet many faculty and occasionally administrators, sponsors, and personnel in government agencies, ministries of education, and foundations believe that young adults should not have to be coddled, that they should have or develop the discipline and maturity to meet their more basic needs by themselves. The discrepancy between these two ways of thinking often makes it difficult to involve faculty in orientation programs. In fact, when students do not receive appropriate reinforcement about the importance of orientation from their faculty, they, too, may adopt negative views. They proceed to explore and discover the new culture by themselves, confident that they have the skills and abilities to do so with little formal preparation.

A recent experience in Indonesia brought this issue sharply into focus. Indonesia's culture is characteristically based on human relationships; it nurtures interpersonal and family-centered values. Despite this, several government officials did not accept the need for cross-cultural orientation to prepare sensitive Indonesians for study in a high-pressured competitive educational setting. They thought the orientation should provide language training and upgrading in the disciplines to the way they were being taught in the United States.

This is an interesting reversal of common American thinking. Instead of providing general cross-cultural orientation, on the assumption that it would lead to improved academic performance, we faced the opposite assumption: that academic orientation in the subject matter enhances educational satisfaction to the point that personal problems do not matter. Research on Indonesian returnees shows they have experienced many problems while abroad, some unresolved, that led directly to more problems upon their return home. But as long as they received their degrees—no matter how long it took—and returned home, their foreign study was perceived as successful, mitigating the case for cross-cultural-orientation program funding. Unfortunately, the studies that provided these insights are unpublished in-house studies, and Indonesian scholars are not usually expected to disclose such problems to their superiors.

The most noteworthy aspect of the Indonesian argument was the recognition that the disciplines themselves were being taught and studied differently in the United States than in Indonesia. This meant that Indonesians arriving in the United States are often perceived as handicapped in two ways: first, by insufficient knowledge in their subject matter compared to their U.S. counterparts; and second, by inadequate training in the cognitive skills normally practiced in these disciplines in the United States. These "handicaps" are serious enough that the Indonesian Ministry of Planning has constructed an achievement test, Test Potensi Academic, which is still in the validating research stage. Preliminary results indicate that subjects scored lower on verbal and analytical sub-scores than the nearest equivalent scores in the United States. The relevant analytical skills require independent thinking, distrust of sources, disinterested scholarship, intellectual skepticism, and ability to defend a point of view—all culturally influenced skills.

From this and many other experiences, it is clear that a different way

169

of looking at orientation is needed. Obviously, students' fields of study are extremely important. But the relationship between academic achievement and orientation has yet to be established in research and in practice.

There are several reasons why academic pursuits should be elevated to a position of dominance. First, they have been neglected even by those who claim to provide it in the form of library tours or academic study-skills training. "General" study-skill sessions are not sufficient, and may in fact be misleading. For example, a mere description of analytical and critical skills probably will not enable a sensitive foreign student to question his or her professor in the open classroom. Most study-skill clinics are designed primarily for undergraduate students who share the same cultural tradition and assumptions. Similarly, taking foreign students on library tours does not interpret the library as a system of problem-solving, concept-forming, and classification that generates knowledge.

It is not surprising that Hoff (1979) found in her study of classroom-related cultural differences that only half of her undergraduate foreign students knew how to use the library properly. Nor have we seen much evidence that study skills are included in orientation programs for U.S. students, whose familiarity with analytical and critical thinking may leave them frustrated or unequipped to deal with the academic system in culturally sensitive or ideologically dominated countries such as Japan, Indonesia, East Germany, or the Soviet Union. This is not to say that training in "general" study skills, presented comparatively and with cross-cultural sensitivity, is useless. Hanvey (1976) suggests that in cross-cultural relations, most contacts are based on a simple understanding of the rules. Without the cross-cultural context, however, students may learn only the "rules" of the academic game but not their meanings. Serious academic study and research require cultural sharing and insight about both the structure and function of a discipline.

The second reason to incorporate the academic discipline is that cognitive skills tend to be discipline-specific (Donald 1985). A discipline is an educational structure with its own internally consistent knowledge, logic, and system of validating and discovering new knowledge. It has its own culturally influenced parts and sub-parts, with unique relationships sometimes understood only by insiders. Disciplinary boundaries indicate where they begin and end, and there are grey areas between them.

Like cross-cultural knowledge, disciplinary knowledge is derived from experiences. But disciplinary knowledge grows from a system of formal rules, called algorithms, and is supported by research, so it is more respected than most cross-cultural experiential learning, which is heuristic in nature. Heuristic learning is commonly criticized as imprecise, spotty, and unpredictable. The lack of symmetry between these two experiential learning systems may explain why many mainstream faculty members, especially in behavioral sciences, are not intellectually active in international student programs, and why they often have ambivalent views about study abroad for U.S. students. It is hard for them to relate these heuristic or personal growth-oriented experiences to their disciplines. There are, of course, "approved" algorithm-based experiences in the disciplines, but they are carefully defined and quality-controlled under various headings, such as laboratories, field work, experiments, or research.

Involving disciplinary faculty in orientation programs for both U.S. and foreign students would enable exchange practitioners to gain valuable insights about the relationships between these two systems of experiences. In addition, it would help internationalize the perspectives of the teaching faculty, because they would need to articulate and provide explanations about the intellectual thought processes of their disciplines. Students often acquire their cognitive skills not by explicit instruction but by early socialization, readings, and implicit reinforcements in the daily use of these intellectual skills (Donald 1985). American students would also benefit from such faculty involvement through improved teaching. This seems valuable, since about half the entering freshmen today do not have the level of cognitive development standard for their age (Donald 1985).

The third reason for focusing on the disciplines in cross-cultural orientation is that the disciplines do have cultural roots. Even so-called hard sciences whose content is universally valid, such as mathematics and biology, have apparent cultural roots in the way they are organized, how their knowledge is being used and disseminated, how their disciplines are viewed by others in the culture, and the way they relate to other disciplines. Including faculty in sophisticated orientation programs for both U.S. and foreign students would help internationalize the disciplines. This in turn would strengthen the study abroad component for U.S. students, which internationally experienced faculty may now be able to relate to their fields of study.

For this reason, a new model is proposed, one that represents all three major variables: culture, learning, and academic discipline. This model is presented in the diagram below in the form of three circles, whose intersections indicate relationships between the variables.

The academic discipline is represented by the largest of three concentric circles (1). The other two circles represent home- and host-country cultures in a comparative perspective (2) and learning theories (3). The second and third circles are smaller to underscore the dominance of the field of study, and to indicate that students do not have to know everything about culture and learning—only those elements that have a direct bearing on their academic pursuits. These necessary elements lie in the overlap between the first and second circles (5), where field of study

171

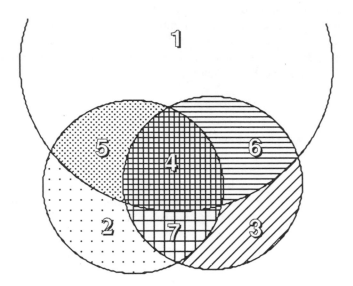

1. FIELD OF STUDY. Knowledge based on the scope and methods of academic disciplines or group of disciplines, including research.

2. CULTURE STUDY. Basic knowledge of the host culture and of cultural principles, including differentiation, understanding of trends and dynamics, and competence with emic and etic perspectives.

3. STUDY OF LEARNING. Relevant theories of learning, including thinking, reasoning, memory, information arrival, problem solving, and other intellectual skills.

4. TRANSFER OF KNOWLEDGE. Competencies from an academic discipline, cultural principles, and cognitive skills that make up the ability to apply, transfer, adapt, and appropriately use knowledge from the host country in the home country. This includes competence of learning to learn, ability to think comparatively, and understanding of multiple goals for individuals, sponsors, families, governments, universities, and home and host countries.

5. CULTURAL VARIABLES OF DISCIPLINES. Relevant knowledge and insight of the cultural variables that influence study and practice of a discipline-based profession in the host culture.

6. DISCIPLINE-SPECIFIC INTELLECTUAL SKILLS. Explicitly acquired relevant knowledge of intellectual and cognitive skills on which the discipline is based.

7. INCIDENTAL LEARNING. Enriched learning and experiences in leadership, management, and general societal functioning as globally interdependent persons.

and culture intersect, and the first and third circles (6), where field of study and learning intersect. The area where all three circles intersect (4) is the all-important transfer point of disciplinary knowledge, self-learning, and self-renewal. Finally, one area (7) falls outside the field of study but links culture and learning. This is "incidental," non-discipline learning, which is related to area (4) but larger, because it reaches into the culture at large. Located here are such competencies as leadership skills in professional associations, or managerial talents in administering functional departments of universities, governmental agencies, or private enterprise.

This scheme relates cross-cultural experiences to academic disciplines and to the role of foreign-educated persons in their own and the host-culture environment; it responds to the call by many educators to develop double (Farnham-Diggory 1972) or even triple specialists. It provides an "ideal type" model to measure orientation goals. It also implies the consequences of ignoring any of these major variables.

How to synthesize and integrate these and related concepts is the major problem facing orientation organizers. We turn to that next.

Synthesis and Integration

Farnham-Diggory (1972) suggested that one of the most important recent theoretical concepts is that people are "cognitive samplers" of constantly changing experiences and stimuli. They continually relate, organize, and reorganize these, receiving and testing the new against the old or currently held. International education is a laboratory with a vastly larger pool of experiences and stimuli than is available in monocultural education, which is the biggest and most obvious advantage to study abroad. If the potential of the study abroad "laboratory" is not fully realized by individuals, it is because they are highly selective samplers. They cannot take the total blame, however; many sojourners compartmentalize their experiences because international education is itself structurally and functionally unintegrated (LaBrack 1986).

If we accept the idea that orientation is a process that lasts throughout the entire experience abroad, then there are many things professionals can do to help individuals synthesize these experiences in order to obtain a fuller benefit for themselves personally and professionally, and to improve international and intercultural relations in general.

Synthesis can be achieved in several ways.

1. The learning environment for international sojourners must be improved to provide a sense of integrated learning. They need to feel secure and accepted, and to sense that there are many facilities available to them as learning and assistance resources as needed.

173

2. Sojourners need the conceptual skills with which to see their experiences from a sophisticated perspective, on a higher level of explanation than as a simple collection of events faced largely by trial-and-error.

3. Sojourners must be encouraged to keep daily records, more like field notes than personal diaries, so they can compare their reactions to experiences over time and find correctives when their heuristic experiences do not match the concepts they have learned. Such notes can also help develop organizing principles with which to handle cognitive overload.

4. Participants should be constantly challenged to recognize the rewarding, satisfying, and creative experiences, which outweigh their problems and difficulties. Research and evaluation provides this list of common positive experiences:

excitement; newness; interesting experiences; never-a-dull-moment; knowledge that international cooperation is possible; constant challenge; enhanced creative solutions; satisfaction when things work; projects and papers get finished; depth of interpersonal relations with faculty advisers, fellow students, co-nationals, host-nationals, and others; gain of self-confidence, ability to function on one's own; constant reminders that things and people are interconnected and interdependent; knowledge that exchangees participate in an important undertaking; feeling of self-actuation; knowledge that participants play a part in a larger scheme of international relations.

Common difficulties include the following:

mental fatigue from constant information/stimulation overload; frustration, anxiety, ambiguity, fears, and uncertainty from daily dynamics of living when no immediate feedback is available; anxiety due to realization of personal ignorance as the extent of what there is to know becomes apparent; encounter with differences and how to deal with them; how to give and receive criticism; seeing one's own culture and country from retrospect; being cut off from normal sources of information and personal and family support, resulting in feelings of loneliness, isolation, and abandonment.

5. Sojourners should be taught how to achieve comparative insights between their home and host countries, and then be provided the rationale for applicability of knowledge transfer from one to the other, with the methods for doing so. Professionals and students should be encouraged to continually explore new approaches, to read and share materials, and to uncover new resources, personally and through professional associations.

6. Participants should be shown the consequences for cross-cultural ignorance, which include:

poor start; delays, longer stay, greater expense; change in degree objectives; chain reactions, increase in difficulties with other problems;

problems caused by seeking too many exceptions, such as alienating faculty advisers and others; more work to overcome later; not being recommended for a higher degree; overall performance lower than optimal or potential; social and intellectual isolation; unhappiness, maladjustment, insecurity; lack of insight about errors, mistakes, problems, thus lacking correctives; failure to use all available resources and poor budgeting of time and financial resources; feeling of being controlled by others or by circumstances; lack of insight about what part of knowledge is applicable in the home country and how maladjustment has an impact on family members and others; greater problems of readjustment upon return home, personally and professionally; failure to provide growth and development opportunities for spouse and children (if applicable); failure to be an effective leader; lack of understanding one's own role in communication and performance; failure to continue in self-motivated and self-learning mode.

Note that most of these items relate directly to the academic part of our model.

7. Sojourners should be encouraged to participate in practical training and job-related experiences. Observations and studies (Lee, Abd-Ella & Burks 1981) show these to be the best-known synthesizers. There is a wide perception, however, that foreign student employment is for financial gain rather than being a way to integrate theory and practice.

8. Most importantly, sojourners should practice applying the same cognitive skills used in their academic disciplines to their entire learning environment. These skills include discussion, questions, disagreements, thinking, doubt, reasoning, new hypotheses, devil's advocacy, and research. Mastery and practice of these skills will also enhance other professional and communications skills. Intercultural living and learning centers, discussion groups, and intellectual activities sponsored by student organizations are potentially the most effective methods of accomplishing synthesis. These skills are the same that support our entire democratic theory and practice; thus, international education makes a significant contribution to the nature of our society and the survival of free institutions, which could not flourish if dominated by bias, self-interest, scapegoating, and hostility toward others.

Some Guidelines and Recommendations

The preceding chapters provide many specific guidelines and programmatic suggestions that relate to the goals, content, structure, sequencing, and methods of orientation. Below is a summary of recommendations, beginning with planning and then addressing specifics of the plan.

Suggested planning steps:
1. Identify the target audience — its demography, anticipated needs, character, training readiness, and prior international experiences.
2. Assess the problems this group is likely to face, based on prior experiences, readings, and evaluations.
3. Anticipate the problems others may have in interacting with this group.
4. Develop immediate, intermediate, and long-term goals, and place all of them into a definitive time perspective, not simply "to be announced" later.
5. Identify the conceptual base on which the new competencies are to be developed. (See Chapter 17.)
6. Determine the competencies to be the focus of orientation and how individuals will know when and whether they have achieved them.
7. Explain instructional strategies and why they have been chosen.
8. Help the students synthesize the materials covered. (See pp. 173-175 in this chapter.)
9. Develop a meaningful evaluation strategy.
10. Identify any research implications of the orientation, and encourage others to conduct research.

Throughout the planning and execution of the program:
- Pay special attention to language and culture.
- Involve a number of others responsibly in the planning and design of the program.
- Enhance your professional standing and respect by providing leadership as an educator, not just as an arranger of sessions. Educate colleagues, faculty, and administration to the potential of orientation to secure cooperation and funding.

Identifying the audience:
- Who needs orientation? All students in or going to a new culture who:
  - wish to succeed in a multiple-track program combining an academic discipline with an international dimension
  - need to increase self-confidence, strengthen self-concept, and gain organized and relevant knowledge of the system
  - recognize the need to function on their own and to practice the principles of self-determination, self-reliance, and independence
  - recognize that they will function in an interdependent world and thus need to gain broader, cognitive perspectives about their future professional careers
  - are concerned about losing their cultural identity in a new culture
  - wish to "hit the ground running" in a new culture
  - wish to enter a new cultural system through a neutral "testing

ground" or, in the case of ESL centers, through a psychological "half-way house" that protects and prepares simultaneously (see Chapter 6)

- have no prior experience with other cultures or are dominated by an exclusive perspective of their home environment
- need to know how people of the host country and other countries think, act, reason, and communicate
- need to gain a higher level of tolerance for ambiguity
- need to clarify their personal and professional goals
- need to understand the nature of their academic tasks
- need to understand the complexity of their host country without being overwhelmed by it
- wish to know when they miscommunicate and how to correct it.

• Needs assessments are important, but they are truly valid only for the specific group for which they are performed. Needs vary between groups and change over time. Professionals should not depend only on needs assessments of the students, but should develop the skills strategic planners use: obtaining materials from outside sources, relevant readings, and information from prospective students' files; and studying demography and trends.

• Exercise special care, cross-cultural insight, and professional judgment in the way the orientation is advertised. Identify expected outcomes. The initial publicity may determine students' attendance and response. Every statement has consequences for their subsequent sojourn.

Goals:

• Identify expected goals. Make explicit the antecedents to the outcomes.

• Orientation goals should consider the goals not only of the students, but also of the educational institution, sponsoring agencies, and other interested and involved parties.

• Place orientation into the larger context of international education, rather than the limited role of "special" assistance for a "special" group whose "special" needs require it.

• All orientation should have short-term, intermediate, and long-term goals, beginning with immediate on-arrival needs and ending with reentry to the home country. Long-term plans should include a variety of enrichment programs designed to enhance substantive experiences rather than support survival groups. Enrichment means adding something to learning, gaining new cognitive skills, or enhancing leadership experiences.

• If transfer of knowledge and learning-how-to-learn are goals of the

177

orientation, they need special attention.
- If you find evidence that overall goals or any part of orientation training runs counter to cultural values, stop immediately to process value conflicts.

Competencies:
- Create an expectation of success in academics, cultural diplomacy, and cross-cultural competencies. The most significant competencies to be gained from an orientation program are ability to:
  - function independently
  - know when, how, and from whom to seek assistance when needed
  - learn how to learn cross-culturally
  - use "natives" as educational resources, including arrangements to study and conduct research jointly
  - motivate one's self to do a variety of tasks that depend on individual responsibility and voluntary choices
  - communicate cross-culturally.

Strategies:
- Once goals are selected and identified, training strategies follow. Be consistent in choosing methodologies congruent with the aims. This is especially important if the goals include assistance with adjustment, academic achievement, cultural relations, or enrichment follow-up programs. Do not try to do everything in a short time.

Strategies pertaining to orientation leaders and resource persons:
  - Include presenters and resource persons from various areas of university and community life, not just "veteran" international students and personnel. Exclusive involvement of persons who have experienced study abroad reinforces isolation and deters students from seeking specialized assistance from other resources. Be sure to involve significant numbers of U.S. students and resource persons for the orientation of international students, and vice versa. This provides assistance to the orientation participants while helping the resource persons to learn themselves.
  - Depending on the goals and objectives, topics should be obtained from disciplines and presenters who:
    - explain as well as describe
    - especially explain the "whys"
    - promote dynamic learning, with some attention to trend rather than a "snapshot" approach
    - facilitate comparative analysis
    - have the cross-cultural communication skills to encourage discussion and doubting

- not only cover the topic at hand but explain the disciplinary perspective from which they speak and the intellectual process involved in their reasoning
- identify the intellectual resources of their disciplines, and explain the role that these disciplines play in our culture.
■ Produce a brief training and informational document for resource persons that explains the roles to be played by all.
■ Clearly communicate to the participants that the organizers and presenters are there not because they are nice, friendly, or dedicated people, but because they have specific, identifiable competencies.

Strategies for sequencing:
■ Goal ordering should be the first activity of cross-cultural orientation, even for the nuts-and-bolts style.
■ Once the individuals' goals have been identified and discussed, explain the university's expectations of the students, so these can be included in the individuals' super-goals. Contemporary critics of higher education often allege that concern with individual choices has become so dominant that we neglect to let students know what we expect of them. These expectations should be presented positively as we explain the needs for international and intercultural education. Students need to know that their education is for the future, that the international component is a unique investment, and that the interest earned from it is the even more unique and still little understood synergy of opportunities.
■ Cross-cultural dynamics, the third item in an orientation, can help individuals understand the various contingencies that may interrupt their sub-goals or divert their attention. This should include a strong emphasis on two key concepts, individual responsibility and utilization of host-country natives as resources.
■ The culture-learning aspects of one's stay —knowing the host and home cultures in comparison—should be the fourth content item. Rather than introducing the host culture alone, the comparative method supports a meta-goal by leading participants to see the importance of associating, living, and learning with members of the host country. A minimum training in cross-cultural communication is needed to accomplish this goal.
■ The development of intellectual skills, especially those relevant to one's academic discipline, should not be part of a separate sequence, but interwoven into all aspects of orientation through discussion, values clarification, and exercises. The methods of training in critical skills include active participation, peer interac-

tion, faculty encouragement, and some form of doubting and questioning. Training in problem-solving includes exercises in which parts are related to the total, concepts are formulated, and inferences encouraged through such questions as, "Why is this occurring?" or "If such is true, then what?" Readings, films, lectures, or discussions should be debriefed for content as well as for cognitive skills employed. Frequent contact with faculty members or professionals in the same discipline is most desirable.

Strategies to increase motivation:
- Orientation should be designed to increase the students' desire for more knowledge through "epistemic motivation." They should leave the program dissatisfied that it ended, wishing they could have had more time to explore the interesting topics. Furthermore, they should have a specific agenda in mind for continuing orientation, some of which they can accomplish through action and readings on their own.
- An additional method for increasing motivation is through use of "manding stimuli" (Wladkowski 1985). Using mands means stressing important points and calling attention to special emphases. Examples include "Please note this ...", "This is an important point that will help you ...", "You will learn more easily if you ...", "Knowing about ... will lessen confusion."
- A little tension in orientation does not hurt if it is the result of exposure to something new that does not fit with established thinking processes or perceptions. Motivation to learn is often enhanced by such tension. Trainers often overdo their emphasis on complete relaxation.

Strategies to enhance learning in general:
- Do not attempt to give detailed answers for all possible contingencies. Unfinished tasks may be better remembered than finished ones.
- Contrary to expectations, preparing students minimally to perform many tasks rather than dealing in depth with a few is not a superficial approach. If international sojourners are the scanners we think they are, they benefit more from a brief introduction to many areas (provided they have the conceptual framework to hang them on).
- When introducing new and unfamiliar material, begin by connecting it to the familiar, because students already have recording and holding skills for such information and know what to expect. Then provide the organizing principles for the new information and, if it is discordant, introduce it with a special reference to that point.

- Do not introduce more than six items of new information at one time without the help of a higher-level concept. Locate the organizing cognitive principles of such concepts and present them in a different mode from the one in which they were originally presented. For example, if a principle is introduced didactically, also present it visually.
- Rules, regulations, and other information or concepts that convey negative or restrictive ideas should be introduced carefully and sensitively. Didactic methods with handouts are usually not sufficient. Use case studies, critical incidents, discussion, comparative analysis of rules, and illustrations of functions that rules play in different societies. Involve scholars of comparative social systems and legal experts.
- Allow time for verbal rehearsal through discussion, repetition, or simulated problem-solving in order to facilitate transfer of information to long-term memory.

Evaluation and research:

Evaluate orientation programs as often as possible. Consider evaluating individual sessions, content, process, presentation methods, and the role of culture in the program.

"You Cannot Do It Alone"

One of the most important keys to succeeding with an orientation program is to place it and yourself in an international context. As Baker has advised, we cannot each do it alone. It is all too easy in an age of obsession with short-term economics to develop a seige-mentality, isolated on our separate campuses and struggling with meager resources and support. It is crucial to tap into the growing stream of orientation activity. Therefore, we make these final recommendations:

- Consider cooperating with other educational institutions in your area or region to create student orientation centers. Sharing of resources is economical, draws on richer resources, attracts larger audiences, and permits practitioners to experiment with new ideas.
- Organize yourselves in NAFSA with others from all sections to discuss orientation issues, produce orientation materials, train, and coordinate programs between host and home countries.

References

Donald, Janet G. 1985. Intellectual skills in higher education. *The Canadian Journal of Higher Education*, 15(1):53 68.

Farnham-Diggory, S. 1972. *Cognitive process in education.* New York: Harper & Row.

Hanvey, Robert G. 1976. *An attainable global perspective: Center for war and peace studies.* New York: Global Perspectives in Education, Inc.

Hoff, Bernardine L. R. 1979. Classroom-generated barriers to learning: International students in American higher education. Ph.D. Dissertation, U.S. International University, San Diego, CA.

LaBrack, Bruce. 1986. Orientation as process: The integration of pre- and post-experience learning. In R. Michael Paige, ed., *Cross-cultural orientation: New conceptualizations and applications.* Lanham, MD: University Press of America.

Lee, Motoko, M. Abd-Ella, and L. A. Burks (edited by S. Dunnett). 1981. *Needs of foreign students from developing nations at U.S. colleges and universities.* Washington, D.C.: NAFSA.

Wladkowski, Raymond J. 1985. *Enhancing adult motivation to learn.* San Francisco: Jossey-Bass.

Contributors

JOSEPH O. BAKER is Chairman of Study Abroad, Brigham Young University.

PATRICIA BYRD is Interim Chair of the Department of English As a Second Language, College of Public and Urban Affairs, Georgia State University.

JUDITH A. CADMAN is Head of Resources and Evaluation Division, Partners for International Education and Training, Washington, D.C.

SUE K. CLARKE is Director of International Studies at Saint Olaf College.

JAN FELSING is Assistant Director for Study Abroad in the Office of International Education and Services, University of Iowa.

SANDRA MUMFORD FOWLER is Head of the Inter-Cultural Relations Program, Naval Military Personnel Command, United States Navy, Washington, D.C. She is also President of the Society for Intercultural Education, Training, and Research (SIETAR).

DARIO GAMBOA is a Consultant in Human Resources in Rio de Janeiro, Brazil. His original paper was written when he was an International Student Adviser at the University of Minnesota.

JOLENE KOESTER is Associate Professor and Chair of the Department of Communication Studies, California State University in Sacramento.

ANN KUHLMAN is Associate Director of the Office of International Programs, University of Pennsylvania.

MARK LANDA is Director of the Program in English As a Second Language, Department of Linguistics, University of Minnesota.

GAYLA MARTY is Senior Editor in the Office of International Education at the University of Minnesota.

JOSEF A. MESTENHAUSER is Professor and Director of the Office of International Education at the University of Minnesota.

ROGER NICHOLSON was at the time of writing Director of Training Support, Office of Training and Program Support, Peace Corps, Washington, D.C. Presently he is Vice President of Nicholson, Dude, Pastore, Luzzatto, and Associates, Inc., Washington, D.C.

JAMES E. O'DRISCOLL is Director of the Office of English and Special Services, Institute of International Education, New York.

HARVEY SARLES is Professor of American Studies, University of Minnesota.

JULIE SOQUET is Director of Orientation and Counseling, The Experiment in International Living, Brattleboro, Vermont.

INGE STEGLITZ was a Fulbright Scholar in Speech Communication at the University of Minnesota at the time of the conference. She then returned to Germany to complete her diploma in Psychology at the University of the Saarland and is now back at the University of Minnesota where she is a graduate student and teaching assistant in Speech Communication.

KAREN ROSENQUIST WATTS just completed her Master of Arts Degree at the University of Kentucky. At present she lives in Washington, D.C.